Jenni Doherty

RAIN SPILL

eve

eve is an imprint of Guildhall Press dedicated to encouraging, promoting and showcasing the creativity of women authors and artists.

Published in November 2012

Guildhall Press
Unit 15, Ráth Mór Business Park
Bligh's Lane
Derry
Ireland
BT48 0LZ
(028) 7136 4413
info@ghpress.com
www.ghpress.com

 Guildhall Press gratefully acknowledges the financial support of the Arts Council of Northern Ireland as a principal funder under its Annual Support for Organisations Programme.

The author asserts her moral rights in this work in accordance with the Copyright, Designs and Patents Act 1998.

A CIP record for this book is available from the British Library.

Acknowledgements

I would like to thank all the dedicated and professional team at Guildhall Press: Kevin, Joe and Declan, and especially Paul Hippsley, who has remained forever supportive and encouraging as an editor, work colleague and friend for the last two decades. Also Damian Smyth, Head of Drama and Literature of the Arts Council of Northern Ireland, for his earnest encouragement to take the next step and for financially supporting this collection.

Further heartfelt thanks due to my wonderful siblings Judith, Daniel, Ronan, Andrew and Olivia; to Saoirse; to the many friends and fellow writers who have encouraged and supported me throughout the decades with special mention to Michael and Dee; Grainne, Eileen, Rachel, Marilyn, Catherine, Felicity, Hazel, Tom and Ursula; Lisa, Tina, Kaye, Kim, Geraldine, Sally, Grace and Stephanie; Kitty, Karen, Lynda, Shirley, Tracy and Liz and all the rest of the BBC Get Writing and More Writing gang; to my lovely former colleagues from the Derry libraries, the Bedlam gang, and of course to Shorty the dog, who has forfeited many a walk when a creative thought has come storming.

Thanks also to all those who have inspired, knowingly or unknowingly, as a friend, colleague, lover or stranger – the words between these pages are due to and for you.

About the Author

Originally from Greencastle, County Donegal, now based in Derry, Jenni's background ranges from publishing, journalism, bookselling and the public library service to facilitating creative writing workshops, organising literary events and performing poetry.

Versions of her work have appeared in the *Belfast Newsletter, Belfast Telegraph, Citizen 32, Derry Journal, Derry News, Hot Press, Inishowen Independent, Inish Times, Irish News, Irish Press, The Orbit, Speech Therapy, Unquiet Desperation, Witsnapper* and *Word Flight* (The Stoners' Press), and broadcast on BBC Radio Foyle, BBC Radio Ulster, Drive 105FM and Inishowen Community Radio.

Other publishing credits include project co-ordinator, editor and contributor to *Moments: Short Stories, Poetry and Drama* (2011), *Wonderful World of Worders* (2007), *EVE... A Celebration of Creative Women* (2006) and co-author of *That Land Beyond* (2003), all published by Guildhall Press.

Jenni currently runs Little Acorns Bookstore and works for Besom Productions Ltd. *Rain Spill* is her debut solo collection and is supported by the Arts Council of Northern Ireland.

To my parents, Daniel and Rosemary,
for giving me love, truth, courage and
belief – thank you.

Inishowen Mist Story

Damp tapestry of landscape
Cool blueness of light
Dewy petrichor of rain spill
Earths me to berth write

Foreword

It is the weather that provides such a familiar, if not somewhat mysterious, backdrop to our daily lives, and in no place more so than in Ireland. Unpredictable, prevailing, relentless – and of course the most topical of conversations – we, to an extent, let it control and determine how we go about our days and nights. Throughout this book you will find various Irish proverbs, in both the Irish and English language, that lend to this belief.

For me, the weather and the elements have been inspirational and integral to the words I choose in what and how I write, although this has never been intentional. Growing up in a small fishing village, living so close to the sea and being surrounded by such a diversity of place and people, adds to the depth of drama and description.

And so, within this collection, I have tried to create the illusion of a water dance through the use of Rain, Ocean, Mist, Fog, Frost, Storm, Snow and Rainbow as metaphors for this sense of place and belonging, of experience and emotion, of life and lessons learnt.

Some pieces have come to be naturally while others have originally been written on a given subject for the purpose of live performance or as topical commentary for broadcast or newspaper. Tender, light and humorous in places yet coarse, raw and unforgiving in others, this is not by any means an autobiographical collection but rather a spill of thoughts, imaginations, fictions, ideas and realities gathered over four decades.

I hope you enjoy the calm and the storm of their fall: welcome to *Rain Spill*.

Jenni Doherty

Contents

STORM

SNOW

RAINBOW

RAIN

Rain is on the way when the dog
nods off to sleep during the day
Agus an gadhar ag míogarnach
i rith an lae tá báisteach air

It will rain when the turf
flame is blue in the fire
Báisteach má fheictear lasair
ghorm as tine mhóna

Rain will fall when the southern
cliffs gasp for breath
Nuair a bhíonn na failltreacha
ó dheas ag sciúgáil sin comhartha
mór fearthainne

Loose Leaves

I am *your* open book
choose a chapter
we may chatter
flatter
group
the pages
in stages
flick through
lick the paper
edge
read softy
slow
then quicken
pace
and race
to poetic
grace
leafing back
curling up
inserting the
place
mark the
fingerprints
of beauty
words
engage my
page and
dip and
pour through
every
crevice
word and

lore
trace the
chase of
secrets
told
the golden
fold
of you
and I
as we
look and
love at
closing
book…

Sunday Ribbons

Filled with the linnet of an August eve
in an '80s border-like town –
Here, less confused with confession-box frown,
where the air was much sweeter,
the beer warm swallowed as words
washed, stirred, swerved and curled
into the swing of a song on a foreign shore –
I stand.

I stand where a Saturday night shawl is like a
bar room belly-danced brawl;
like Deadwood;
like a Bosch painting in the tropics or
Brueghel: a rough, crazy-cut dart of a diamond shot.
Yes, *hear*, I stand.

But, something calls ye home:
that scent of dusk;
a whispered doorway charm;
the brush of midnight blues
on jazz of cities true
where tempt of corner streets
let secrets spill in heat;
where haunts of other towns and
beggars, buskers, clowns
remind you once of Wilde and youth and
where ye used to be...

A nostalgic nudge.

Smudged memories of what could have been,
should have been –

a twitching switch of dreams on screen,
a reel of girlish glee and screams.

Aye, I was bold then.
Bowled over then.
It was the music, the mood, the company, the world;
word on word making sense.
making sentences,
making out,
making love…
breaking free.

We remember hideaways and doorstep gropes,
giggle winks and daisy trees.
Remembered love and life and, oh,
how we laughed and learned
to somersault with cider draught
with skin and tongue assault
on whim to spin on body craft.

Intrigue: a meeting of minds,
an honesty hum.

A past released
eavesdropped on poetic edge –
pulled warm from rain;
stunned wet with sin;
a promise touch of something more –
an echoed voiced encore.

Love was the thing that woke up,
that spoke up,
in the middle of the night,
lit a cigarette bright and burnt them bastards down.

Love was the flame licking shame of bullets hired,
of fired hearts, beating the odds,
no shot for alarm.

Love was,
was Love.

Give us time.
Give us hours to twilight such unspoken crime.
Us babes in the wood,
mere sketches of shadowed kin,
our ashes in moons strip rainbows
stunned far out on strings of stars.

Have us trust.
Have us thrust the rush of blushes,
the curse of crushes, and
spike barbed wire hushes
to moist a choice of lust.

We are born of lands and many hands.
We are stretched and fetched through
illustrious histories and lore.
Touched with the shorthand of our nerves,
stories, imaginations score –
in the middle of nowhere,
at the circle of everything;
at delicate salty crusted core.

I stand seduced by earthly smells,
drown in its colour of truth.
I want to keen and howl.
I want to embrace all this and surface hot with clay.
I want to bury my fingernails deep to dig out

taunt of ancestral call and
I *will* love my unborn children
more than them.

**

It's Sunday,
on the bridge of an afternoon not quite sold.
A different time.
Different soul.
December rain.
Coffee cup still warm.
Cigarette tilted; a neon tip on pen nib felt.
And, I smile.
Smile at the very thought of all this at half-hung door.
Chilled with the fillet of such fragile bones –
a salmon of knowledge on past;
a river of ribbons spun to sting into love,
a skeleton *sceal* of scales not yet told.
To be hooked, caught, unravelled –
and, by God and country –
clasped and bold, once more.

Donegal Doorstep

Braided boulevards and luscious lanes,
shore paths born for lovers.
thin summer frocks bathing sweet shoulders
rainbow flowers still stolen hours.

Pin-striped lawns in the womb of late afternoons,
dogs laze at backdoors of matchbox houses.

Castle ruins laced with history, entwined with moss,
could marry or have a wild affair with its loveliness.
Stones bright in flames though melt with snow,
hold precious wishes and special kisses
then leave their jewels to rot in the rain.

Neighbouring windows hold secrets of lives.
People moving through blue dusks and dawns.
Evenings swathed in pink gloom of fallen sun –
A colour vain old women light their room.

The screech and squall of sneaky seagulls,
spying on fisherman's catch of the morn.
Fishing fleets float by like last autumn's leaves –
Bold boats chained to the sea,
drunk on season breeze.

A thread of cross-water blobs –
Prison dots like baby oranges,
flirt and fight with the friendliness of the Foyle.

Rocks stand undisturbed in silent dignity,
waves caress; crash against their souls.
Screaming, protesting, teasing and torrid,
tumbling, turning as it tides and folds.

Ecstasy in union, rhythmical sounds.
Fountains of spring, damp granules of sand.
Grey skies like pale patchwork dreams,
faded denim frothed at the seams.

A treasure trove of thoughts, troubles and tears.
A language of love, life and laughter.
A place of peace, pride and penance.
Where dreams are
realised, released and remembered –

Yes, this is my village opening doors.

Legenderry

Where ancient meets modern beyond spirit and stone
Where river walks and rich parks charm to the bone
Where streets burst with colour and shopping galore
Where music and magic pulse proud to the fore
Where fine food and drink stir, tempt and impress
Where culture and knowledge challenge and address
Where artists of all attitudes entertain and enthral
Where strangers become friends
on the banks of the Foyle
Where voices are choices that inspire and spin gold
Where generations of celebrations are
breathtaking and bold
Where language and heritage, the craic and the *ceol*
Open up to all nationalities as centuries fall
These stories and glories lie in wait for your hand
So come visit, come sparkle, to our legendary land.

Cara

We stood
You stared
I whispered
Nervous words
Tripping kisses

We touched
You smiled
I laughed
Near 6:00am
'Neath army shoulder

We watched
You sighed
I moaned
From cobbled walls
A Tuesday yawning

Fresh fingerprints
Old age in sleep
Bird tasting chips
On Bogside silence

Last cigarette
Then secret spark
Like matches struck:
We clicked.

Secret Town

There were barbed-wire friendships –

bombed on beer glass bold, tough pockets of past,
stolen smiles, those mad-torn memories.
History in our bones, stained, soiled in skin,
blood boiled, toiled and troubled,
slipping sunken on iron streets,
erupting with arms in stones, bitterness and love.
Hands-in-hands becoming fists,
that bashing boom with coiling smoke –
Dirty old town by the Gasyard wall.

We were like fugitives –

singing nerves, ordered songs,
racing through huddled back ways,
grounds of broken windows, concaved car carcasses.
A yawn of brakes, the snore of diesel combustion,
the wakening town stretching, trembling, shivering near.
Pavements bristling with static,
thin thundering lips, broken river mouth,
seeking refuge with fresh explosion,
bullet-bullied words, and
mouthfuls of black rain spluttering,
spitting, bursting curse. The air;
a tissue shredding frost promises,
cool chill slicing, mincing thirst.

And us –

Flitting from bar-to-bar, bed-to-bed,
eyes mirroring traffic lights of green, orange yet
red with tears and anger.

Night tightening its grip on throated thought,
letting rip cries of passion, pleasure, pain.
Then doorstep grope, street wolf-whistle, mad-dog bark,
haunt and moan of Rosary chant:
Holy Mary Mother of God…
Pausing to light a cigarette,
chips mixed with curried caution,
linking arms, warming faces by burnt-out shell of
Ulster Bus.

And I –

with fired girlish hands –
pray, touch, kiss all goodbye…

Falling Rain

Sean descended the cobblestone steps to the eerie water, now tinselled with twinkling frost. He could see waves caressing the rocks. Ecstasy in union. Rhythmical sounds. Utopia. This was power. This is power. Water was stronger than life. Water was stronger than flesh.

The plunge sent waves circulating for a few seconds, yet the next smacked the rocks as before. Towering bullies crashed against these vast victims, who stood undisturbed in silent dignity and indifference. They had stolen another innocent loner. A life. A beauty. A youth. But he was free. He was home.

It started to rain again...

Rain Spill

Voice of Guinness; pouring, soaking
velvet stroke of strolled tongue roll.
Raining soulful, sensual, smooth drawl,
strumming, humming, gorgeous coil.

Secret fingers tap on heartstrings,
kissing quavers, crocheted curls.
Pull me under, over, chord me,
singing words of dew-dropped pearls.

Voice of coconut, milked with honey,
seeping, swollen, churning, hot,
spilled delicious, gold dust whispered,
oiling spoil of juice words shot.

Play me laughing, gentle shoulders,
stung on string of drenching notes.
Curve me cradled,
gee-tar straddled,
breathless storm of ballads sought.

Hungry verses feeding lovers,
slick and husky, curse of song.
Beauty brilliant, thirst of friendship,
deep throat tender,
night goes on...

Village Buttons

You come out from under the bare tree where you were sheltering and you only realise how cold your hands are when you cup them to light a cigarette and the flame from the last pub match doesn't scorch your fingers. The mountains around you are gleaming like glasshouses as the sun comes out again. Trampled grass springs back up; a trail of bubblegum and eucalyptus leaves follow you.

Memories hold onto whatever the wind howls up and hurls at them, the same way that a barbed-wire fence clings to cellophane sandwich wrappers or a scrap of sheep's wool. A couple of cowherds munch magic mushrooms when they aren't delousing each other. These are truffles, tiny things, but they are letters of an alphabet that the memory inscribes in its silences.

I am here watching with the mountains and the sky. Listening to the roar of the sea, the ebb and flow of its consistency to this particular shore, the constant self and me. Waves carry the hum of fishing fleets to the very edge of my being. Seagulls dance overhead, twirling and turning in union. Spitting and squawking, disturbing the swish of water slap on sand. I call back this place where I grew up and will further grow. Inishowen; my Tír na Nóg, my Land of Eternal Youth – wild, barren, brutal, enchanting landscape. Wild, bold, brilliant escapism. Mine. All mine.

Those velvet mountains heavily draped in heather, glorious pageants of colour protecting me. Sleepy towns with streets stretched out like tired elastic, and drama; a word that best describes this sweep of ruggedness and the lives of the people who live here. I surrender myself to this once more.

Here exists a history, the past, my past. The history of moments that we occupied when we were children splashing in puddles, or as friends laughing, running through fields, then lovers hugging and making out in mossy castle ruins. Moments that we all once shared, stolen, lost or could always return to. I have returned.

I've come a long way from those envious, fumbling days of adolescence, those bittersweet memories of schoolgirl antics and first teenage snogs. A long way from innocence; reading comics, riding bicycles with the wind in our hair, skipping school, swapping stories, gathering conkers, staining fingers with blackberries, sneaking cigarettes, skimming pebbles into the sea, sharing secrets and hanging out.

No matter what you've done, no matter how you've changed, to everyone else you are still the skinny, dark-haired, freckled girl with the top button of her shirt tightly fastened who collected shells and liked to write. The girl who was the first to wear Doc Martins. The girl who put washing up liquid in her hair to make it stand up and got caught in the rain. The girl who believed in fairies and sipped cider. The girl who was shy and read Judy Blume. A shadow of her older sister. The spit of her older sister but with a smaller nose. Smaller bum. Bigger smile.

Then there were the fishery boys she had silent hopeless crushes on. There were the village boys she had noisy equally hopeless crushes on. And then there was him. The boy from a neighbouring town. That beautiful, raven-haired, blue-eyed boy. He was hers then. First love. Now, long gone. That was seventeen years ago…

**

Now home for a summer weekend. The height of August regattas; magic midnight swims, busy barbecues, beach parties, ice-cream strolls through the village green and the grand festival end in the seaside marquee – live music, dancing, laughing and drinking until dawn. Voices and glasses twinkling over the sensual sounds of the sea. And I am here with brothers and sisters, friends and neighbours. Massed ranks of former peers; old adversaries, old lovers, old school pals. An amorphous, indistinguishable group; a strange bonhomie descends over all.

The peculiar sense that although all these people appear different; changed in style, maybe a little heavier, wrinklier, greyer – they are all in fact exactly the same as they used to be. This should be reassuring but somehow it isn't. It's strange. Time has stood still as I stand and watch. I watch and stand then take a deep breath, head up, pint in hand and put the best Doc-foot forward.

I am sucked into greetings right and left, big hellos and squeals of recognition. I can remember a time when we all knew everything about each other from the innermost secrets of our pencil cases to whether we'd moved on to French kissing yet. I find myself lost for words, shy again and sixteen. I fiddle with the top button on my shirt once more. Ghosts of the past with different hair-dos and lip-sticked mouths meet me, cashmere or tee-shirt clad, with G&Ts or pints of Guinness.

All around me similar potted histories are being recounted: been here... fifteen years, same job, same place, same boyfriend, getting married, three kids, one dog, a goldfish...

Which job? What boyfriend? How many fish? Too late. Someone else is greeted. We spill our souls and decade summaries to one and all. Village pleasantries exchanged, hands shook, gentle hugs. And gossip. We chatter about the only things we really have in common – the past.

And it's back to the time I got drunk, climbed onto the school roof, fell off and broke my leg. The time I got caught smoking in the toilets at school and was suspended for a week. The time I threw up in Mass at Ballybrack over Mrs Gillen's new tweed jacket during Communion. The time I was overheard cursing in class and had to write a 500-word essay on life as a ping-pong ball, and in French. The time we chased cows who then chased us and we ended up swamped in cowpat. The time before I was really me.

Who was I? Was that really me? Who am I now? The problem is that I'm not so far away from all these terrible reminiscences that they have lost their sting. Perhaps I haven't changed as much as I'd like to think.

We talk much, gradually feeling at ease and drinking in that little bit more. We settle into our little dotted groups and cheer each other on. The mood changes. The smile beckons. The interest is genuine. I begin to remember that all those memories are not bad ones, and instead of raking up nightmarish episodes, we start to recall all the funny ones, too. The time we bought cheap bottles of beer, borrowed guitars, made a fire and had a singsong on the beach for the Gardaí to arrive and discover we were all under-age (was grounded for a month). The time we went skinny-dipping in the moonlight at Sweet Nellies only to have our clothes pinched and catch a cold.

Then discussions about our respective futures, barely imaginable, but so desperately longed for. That shared discovery, the camaraderie, our hopes and dreams bubbling forth. How are your parents, the children? How are we? How are you? Who's still about, who's still alive, who's passed away? We must meet up. We should see much more of each other. Not in a great group but as individuals so we can talk and get to know each other once again. We owe it to our memories… And with top button unfastened, I smile in agreement.

Suddenly life seems full of lost opportunities and squandered friendships. Old friends like new shoes. Promises to be more than Christmas-card scribbles. You must meet the partner. Meet the kids. View the new house. Let's make a day of it. Anytime. Drop by for coffee. Would love to see you again. Bring your man. And soon.

I hear the echo of former gallantry. I sense an intimacy recaptured. I feel a welcoming warmth. The village backdoor is always, always open. So, come on in. And it reminds me, like nothing else, of the girl I used to be and oddly enough home would not be the same without it.

This is where I want to be.

OCEAN

The shrill oyster catchers bring
wet and windy days
Fliuch gaofar is na
roilligh ag éagaoin

When foam makes white roads in
the sea, bad weather will come
Doineann má bhíonn cúr ina bhóithríní
bana tríd an bhfarraige

If there is good visibility at
sea, bad weather is coming
Droch-chomhartha ar muir an
léargas a bheith go maith

Candle Facts (Flexing The Exes)

Every year I lit a candle
for my birthday
'til I was twelve,
entered life with torch above me
shone my beacon on worldly shelf.

Met more candles in shapes of boyfriends
melted warm within their glow,
slowly scorching, wafting perfume,
tapered fiery against their form.

Traced my shadow in their spotlight
smouldered deep beneath their gaze,
gently flickered, bending backwards
lit up golden by licking blaze.

Burned 'til morning
when wick had finished
then so softly blowing out,
let them fall and wax forgotten
silhouettes of former doubt.

Now I'm thirty, no more candles,
have replaced with electric bulb.
Turn the switch on, not as brilliant,
yet, this is my lightning love.

Six Years Later

Can there be a new beginning with every word and
its six years' weight?
Softly, we hold our places, our faces,
lost in the aim of unknown direction,
brilliant eyes in flight among people.

We knew long evenings wet with youth,
first love and lasting laughter.
Those blue eyes made the air pulse
electrify all around and me.
Those star-studded teeth rip open my heart
like lightning.
Your face like the break of new mornings.

I rehearse your echoes.
Inscribe your words.
Devour your energy.
Cherish your gifts.
Paint your smiles.
Retrace your footprints.

A last check between me and my first glimpse of you –
The rush of feelings six years later.

Can we rekindle old flames and
warm in wombs of late afternoons?
I am the same girl, yet,
I yearn for the stream and its reeds
which once knew us happy.

When I lie awake beside your silence,
I ache as you sleep,
caught in dreams and tomorrows.

Each morning tastes of thinking of you.
And sometimes above rain and city noise
I listen to my voice say, *I love you*.
And sometimes above rain I curse the day we met.

The River

I am the same girl yet I yearn for the stream and its reeds
which once knew us happy

Take me to that river…

That secret blue-screamed dreaming stream
where stirring stars lick curve of night
cool crickets click in tricky grass
flies waltzing clear of spider trance
and distant dogs dark bark of home.

First our footsteps shred glass-cut leaves
we drink in haunts of stretch-drenched earth
then damp in longing, calling song
pluck tender stalks to suck out sap
tongues fed, sweet promise, seeking throne.

Break me to a shiver…

Past the Castle,
wooden rusty bench,
we carved our names with coins in June
and water lapped on naked soles,
twined soulful berthed on sandy warm
wet bedded, seaweed threaded tread
salty mix, broke loose, unshelled,
pursed free fresh clam
all pink and moist, revealing pearl
I swam to you,
you gave to me,
my drunken sailor,
this mermaid true.

Make me want to quiver…

When we spun like woven wreaths of reeds
entangled, golden strung,
twisted thighs on clustered clover
flushed,
voices hushed,
anointed with honeyed dew
blossomed through,
scent spiralling,
curlew,
starling,
come back,
pierce my wing,
have our lips, hot skin rekindle
beauty spring.

Let us tremble in those rushes…

Desired dawn 'til midnight spent
bodies cashed on mud-bank rent,
stolen, damp in evening womb
to love once more, become undone
and come again with wind and rain.

Yes,
I am still that girl
who yearns for deeds that knew us then.

God,
just let me go,
to drown at last and
breathe again…

Window Of Iris

Wet windows like ice cubes
twinkle indigo in June,
spilled squares with soft secrets
of other lovers' rooms.

Graze graceful silk curtain,
chiffon dusk, chiselled dawn.
Stemmed youth, ebbed and flowing
on crystal crest morn.

A splash of juiced-jazz sounds
bold bedside spread bare,
on shore of schemed-dreamers,
damp heat, violet dare.

Raised sails from the fast-flesh,
then calm tilting storm,
tongues liquid-lip-linger
pure passion, plumed-sworn.

Those turquoise-stoned eyes
wide open like sky,
navy my dew thoughts
in shades of deep dye.

Your pools are then anchored
on hazelnut true,
inject me with colour:
that cool soulful blue.

Facelift

Do you ever catch yourself in the elevator metal shine,
think altered images and notice stray eyebrow crime?
See how wrinkles and pale face look smooth and tan,
then step out on fifth floor and catch your foot in the jam?
Do you ever then swear that you'll go home and pluck,
or rather, next time, take the stairs and duck?
I do, sometimes, but I always forget,
'cause at least I've still got eyebrows
so I'll not worry yet.

Passioned Pint

Drink from me…

Take a sip from this hour-glass grace
let me stay with you moist,
to glisten below your soaking stare,
then swish and swallow,
sluice-steady,
loose,
ready,
then slowly
let me set within
your perfect patient swim,
that think-tank, sink-sank
sensational serve.

Sway your hips for more golden glow,
wanting much of this liquid kiss,
wet leisure drenched on sanguine lips –
that full-bodied flavour –
such sweetness a little birth-bitter,
just sensually savour,
but a taste too delicious
thirsting on your tongue.

Do not spill or waste…

Let me warm your spirit,
cooling with an ebb and flow,
swirling, swerving, swelling down,
deep down…
While washing you I bow,
still pouring, exploring, lower.
And yet, you desire so much more,

and I, too…
This, my lasting order,
as love's distilling orgasmic cure…

Seductive Smoke

Lift me gently from the pack,
crafted fingers on my back.
Strike me,
spark me,
light me up;
do not drag,
or make me stop.

From your lips I hang on words,
curling-twirl in blue-hued haze.
Let me cling and bring you curse,
surrounding you in haloed gaze.

Inhale me,
exhale me,
don't jail me for health.
You need me,
desire me,
your weakness –
my stealth.

I am always lingering,
tempting,
flickering near.
I will breathe for you,
seethe for you,
come on, cowboy,
you've nothing to fear.

I am there for your distressed caress,
I will not burn you or ever confess.
So roll me, then
troll me,

drag on me hard.
Don't crush me,
dare flush me or
leave me uncharred.

Because you've had it.
You're an addict.
You're my wonderful choke.

So, suffer on, little dahlin',
caught in the clutch of my
seductive smoke-stroke...

Sticky Fingers

It's her mouth – pouting, but not coral pink – that Tony sees first. He feels spied on, sort of shelled. A fleeting, darting feeling ripples through him as he blushes on a stumble of words.

'Fish need feeding.' Schlooooop!

So many sucking Os blink on the humming surface, setting water bubbling. Tiny, all-seeing things gobble the fleshy pads of his fingertips, and from there to his guts something shoots. Gorgeous electricity, deep and delicious. Julie lifts her eyes. Dark blue-green to his pale blue-grey. Bluey-greeny-greyish-blue. And next to the gurgling aquarium, with sticky fingers, he turns and kisses her; floating.

Occupational Hazard

Oscar was so looking forward to the Sea Monsters' Saint Patrick's Day Ball. He had been practising for weeks but in his rush to get dressed he had forgotten his violin. He knew what would happen next. He'd be put on percussion and he hated that stupid xylophone.

'Damn these octopus tentacles,' he scowled. 'I may as well get legless…'

My Funny Valentine (Or April Fool)

Aren't men funny? Unfortunately, not always.

When all is said and done, and it has been lately, funny men are the most attractive men in the world. Magically, funny doesn't fade; most other attractions seem to – haven't you noticed?

Okay, I'm not talking Paul Newman eyes, Brad Pitt looks or Jim Morrison bod (in his prime) – they're one-offs. Maybe they've never really had ugly looking or ugly feeling days in their lives. It's just possible that I'd have looked for laughs elsewhere if I could have spent life with Paul (too old), Brad (too taken), Jim (too buried), but they were always busy and they live there and I live here, you know how it is. Shame really, might have liked the Hollywood life, the Hollywood wife; life without laughs, but looks…

I find I'm watching the men on the screen very critically for signs of physical deterioration. You think this sounds like male sexist patter coming from a woman? Well, physically attractive is what they're selling and physically attractive is what I'm meant to be buying, and I'm not complaining (yet) but for how long can I be entertained?

A six-pack and a smooth back aren't always the top spot for me; they're a bonus, of course but I don't want to be upstaged down the supermarket in the rush to purchase the latest magical cosmetic product for perfection. (That's *my* job – isn't it?) The exterior packaging may well be drop-dead gorgeous, but I want that inner charm and something a little bit more than a coveted/converted accessory hanging off *my* arm.

Yes, there are some who say that good humour is one of the very best articles of dress you can wear in society, and in that they don't mean hideous. Look, listen up, lads – go easy on the circus shirts, the stone-washed jeans and the Moses sandals, please. We have our own wardrobe to contend with and it isn't funny. No, it's not.

As a self-confessed dedicated follower of a passionate – as well as irrational – fashion, I want to be impressed as well as caressed. You've got to make me laugh. Make my sides ache. Find my funny bone and infect it. Spread that desirable disease and cause an epidemic.

Laughter is the modern fashionable drug. It's true to say that once you experience it, you're hooked – not a dry-out clinic or dry eye out in sight. It is an addiction worth having and it's free. Let's legalise it. Let's laugh at ourselves and make others laugh. It's contagious, and boy, oh boy, is it sexy as hell.

You meet someone. That love-at-first-sight (and bite a little later?) builds tension. Laughter releases it. Shared laughter gives an instant rapport. It's therapeutic. It helps you relax. Being relaxed means your defences are down, and smiling makes you look more attractive – when a girl has pretty teeth she never fails to see a joke – plus, it encourages eye contact; maybe not Newman's eyes, but any man's eyes will do (if they're open).

To be honest, it is the laugh in our men – not the men in our life – that will keep us girls chuckle-buckled and alive. To heck with seducing minds and finding souls and g-spots and pretty faces – a guy that can have us splitting our sides scores hands down, bottom's up, every time. So, rather than trying to charm the pants off us, guys, just concentrate on some good wholesome harmless chat instead. It will beat the giggle-wiggles out of us, of that I can assure you.

But then, why is it that there seems to be an alarming shortage of men confident enough and/or wise enough to be funny? Maybe some of them just don't have that rare perception and outlook on life? Maybe others are more self-absorbed, or repressed, and less aware of the absurdity of one's everyday existence? Where are all these raiders of the lost lark hiding out? It has indeed become a temple of doom, I'm afraid. No mills and bloom; no thrills and swoon…

Have we all become too serious, too selfish and too desperate? Where's that twinkle of *bonhomie jolie*? Or are some of us just gagging for a little French (or whatever nationality) tickler and that *je ne sais pah-ha-ha* to end with a 'bless me, blether, for I have grinned'?

And why is it that women who are funny do not always know they are and men who think they are funny, just aren't?

Why do some men tell the same jokes again, and again and ag-ony-ain? Here, I rest my chase. Women in the company of other women generally have a laugh and yes, a little because we are discussing men. (I may as well be honest here. They do occupy our minds, now and then.) Men are great material to discuss and cuss, although, in saying that, we are not all materialistic or fabricating the issues. It does work both ways. It isn't gender exclusive. Being funny is interactive and everyone needs a little elbow encouragement and knee-jerk reaction. It's all in the timing: the knowing when, how, what and where. The *why* comes later.

Why? Because I do know that there is someone out there: that wonderful, drooling fool. They might be funny looking, but I don't care. As long as they are funny within, that's what counts – mind you, it helps if they brush their teeth, wash their socks, leave the bins out and know what a spatula is.

The best thing about being with that funny man is that when there is humour sprinkled liberally across life you don't taste the bad bits. A funny guy gets into your system (where the vain and beautiful one gets into your bathroom and steals your face packs) and he stays put.

Really, I don't always expect a man to make me laugh, but I do want one with a sense of humour and who can tickle my fancy. And if I make him laugh and he asks me to bed and I turn him down? He should laugh it off, say he was only kidding and promise not to hold it against me. Well, not tonight anyway...

Basically, Girls Just Wanna Have Fun and we want it now. We want that funny man who can make us laugh when we've been stung on the lip by a wasp or managed to break that precious antique vase from his adorable mother. (Look, it didn't match the curtains anyway.)

We want that funny man who can forgive us when we've given him two sleeping pills instead of aspirin. (Could have been worse; could have been the dog's worming tablets.) The funny man who will understand completely when we've turned his shabby, most prized, football shirt into a dishcloth. (Of course he had outgrown it, years ago.)

I never thought I'd say this, but it is the naughty noughties and I'm in the market for casual laughter and I'm going to giggle around. I'll be wonderfully relaxed – chuckling over burnt beans on toast and a cheap bottle of plonk. I won't feel rejected if he doesn't phone after bouts of uninhibited guffaws – he's probably on his way over with a bunch of puffy dandelions.

Humour is the cup on the saucer of character. I'm no mug but I do live in hilarious hope for my cup to overfloweth with mirth and I'd rather die laughing (and broke) than live bored (and loaded.)

Really, I'm not asking too much: a Billy Connolly, Spike Milligan, Woody Allen, Bill Hicks, Peter Cook and Jack Dee all rolled into one? One for all and all for one? (That one being for me.)

I fancy a game for a laugh and a joke with a poke, plus in our lifetime, no-one's going to suggest Safer Laughter – or are they?

So, send in the clowns, the funnies, the jokers and knee-jerks and come up and see me sometime. I'm home every evening, dahlin'…

MIST

A garden around the moon
means rain soon
Garraí na gealái – baisteach

A white mist half way up a hill is
a sign of sultry weather to come
*Brothall – fionncheo ar
thaobh an chnoic*

When the mist on the
new moon dies of thirst,
dry weather is in store
*Is dual do cheo gealái
úire bás a fháil ón tart*

5:12am

Lovers and insomniacs,
keepers of the secret hours –
tilt your heads and listen,
hush now, glisten...

For the swish of curtain soul
tugs strings open, spilling all
tilted ledge of paint-stripped heart
pained and pinned,
erotic, smart.

And those velvet folds of night,
satin shapes pull cashmere fall,
draws to cotton sheets of morn
clean and bright as flesh reborn.

Yet my spells are dreamed away
in harsh corduroy of day,
but I shall sleep to wake again
live like ghost-lace to touch you then...

Skin Shadows

Such story-stung stares
tongue me your scorn,
I listen, I linger,
'til murmuring morn.

Cool watered nights' tattoo
dust-dusky charm notes,
a song on bare shoulders
strung out to stir hopes.

A drop into spill
of midnight bruised blue,
stun sleepwalking stars,
jazz smash me to you.

Lust was the secret that
stoked us last night,
lit cigarettes red,
burnt finger tips bright.

I sipped on your voice,
you shipped on my sound,
roguish lilt of soft brogue,
southern drawl trawling found.

Un-spooled like fine sliver
from knit of spooned moon,
sin crocheted some girl's curves
curled under your skin.

You've pinned other lovers
to your scarlet-smart bed,

they pined to be mothers,
yarn long from your stead

to break, shiver shake,
your birthmark purled scar;
unlock, quiver shock,
your gorgeous scowled heart.

Yet, inside my everything
nothing pulls me out more:
your stalk starching promise
your darn scorching score.

So, remind me of something,
bind me to your scold,
spin me your language,
embroider me bold.

Stitched brilliant and tangled
sewn into your core,
unravelled, thread-travelled
at every torn hour.

But a-frayed and a-fragile,
sin-suality incensed,
we'll never skin shadows
nor dare to silk quest...

Distraction

I want you to do to me what you do to words:

Touch poetic edge of sensual soul
snap branch of thunder thought
taste silent rain- rivered stun
storm language twisted spin
burst hypnotic stare
erotic harmonised dare.

Have you scrawl black velvet strokes
story write hot skin,
bury lyrical within
I, woman –
You, man –
stoned sin stilled curse,
beautify butterfly curl,
taunt dragonfly purse.

Fire those prose pearls of

love, footsteps, sleep,
scent to burn,
shell, spill, swamp –
hung, sung,
stung into flesh.

Then curved tongues –
spooned delicious, scooped ambitious,
unhinged room
whispered windowsill bare to
swing on shore, seagull roar
swell-crush core...

And barefoot in your mind –
street canvas bound.

Sprint perfect print to
drench your senses page,
soak seaweed scroll,
stoke salty sage,
lick thy spine,
pluck sweet shrine, in thyme,
cool cornered crime.

Do to me –
secret sounding sword, whipped dagger torch –
scorch this thirst.

Let me be the first to jazz your muse,
spirit through dewdrop dance,
starved hungry feeding chance.

Desire I, your score
inspire my mind pour:
to drip, sip, deeper,
darker, devil more.

Yes –
floor-whored with wishing, wanting,
your word on mine...

Gypsy Kissed

I kissed you

After midnight
in silent stare of rain.
And that moment –
Sheltered lust,
pursed in moonlight –
You clasped then twig-teased
under soaking Oak.

I choked on thought
of what
I'd do to you,
you'd do to me,
me on you,
you in me
stalk-thundered through.

I kissed you

But it meant little.
You wouldn't listen.
Your hot tongue glistened,
skin cashed suspicion,
limbs lashed in mission,
such secret bristlin'
sold out to sin.

I kissed you

Lies thieving truth.
Slick dirty meeting
smart cheatin' sprung,

two-timing torso;
one muscled wrong.
You hung a winked mock,
sardonic glare,
no shock of foreplay
filth-guiltied dare.

I kissed you

A bargain fuck-it.
Eyes: coppered coins
loot bruising cursed slot.
Loins pounding well-spent,
trans-action gage,
on loan for quick rent
a sterling rage.

But *was* it special:
seductive shame,
much more than duty –
fast, wild, insane?
A cheap engagement
exposing sound,
no caution auction
Us: Lust & Found?

Should've been beautiful
and just for us –
Something frail, imagined
like jewelled entrust.
Barely hidden yet starkly seen,
but I twisted it
to an ugly thing,
furtive sword
your fragile chord,

whoring back
unjust reward.

I kissed you

But since you'd paid me –
The kiss was void.

Hooked

Trepping through dark wet marsh with
only the moon as guide,
every sound and shadow heightened,
trespassing beyond the norm,
excitement and fear triggered curiosity,
the pull of pure adrenalin.
And all this before you even cast your line.

Hours pass like minutes.
Thought free while dodging bats flying low,
frozen fingers untangling line,
supping coffee from a flask,
being at one with the night and its creatures,
no words need be spoken,
on fire with the rush of a splash,
an anticipated bite,
the triumph of a silver bar.
Then coming home while the rest of the
world lies sleeping.

There is no comparison to this.
An adventure and assault on the mind and body,
fully absorbed into the atmosphere;
fully absorbed in you.

Black Magic

Now naked from her golden gown, would she be that chosen one to melt delicious on his tongue?

She lay there waiting, smooth and silky with curves of glossy dark. So subtly perfumed; such elegant decadence and desired by all. It only took a moment for him to devour her completely, her dusky tempting truffles irresistible.

'Fancy another?' the confectioner teased.

Now Or Never

Whitewashed buildings, with small blue-shuttered windows, stunned streets, steeped like staircases. A honeycombed maze led through low arches to blind, hidden corners where marauding Turkish pirates once had boiling oil poured on their heads. A world of its own, a life folded in on itself, a clenched stone fist.

It was then that he asked her, 'Will you marry me?'

Strange String Fellows

His viola-curved love sought her violin purr

her honey-milk skin
her calligraphy scrawled hair
the full sting of her butterfly mouth

her eyes, bright brown moon-tilts
pure gold-leaf tipped
her voice;
like dewdrop stir on insect's wing

her words:
delicate pencil shavings
well carved and clear

her laugh;
storm on cheek
touch of shell
strip of silk

His viola-curved love sought her violin purr
but all she wanted was to bang the drum.

The Curse Of Sweet Cyber-ability

You –

An asterisk on my stapled heart,
a hyphenated line from my paper-clipped brain
punctuated my every chaptered move,
fowled my vowels and imperfected verse.

Didn't block me with stops or bullet-point stress
you gave me space and large capped-caress,
served many months of wordy sentence with you –
an A to Z life book of lyrical confess.

You gave me an introduction
to sign the dotted line,
didn't blank or dared delete me
but touch-tendered my form.

Then serialised my wanting
duty-described its thrust,
superscripted my yearning
conversed my muse in trust.

I was that patient comma,
sharpened my colon, compass point,
dotted those eyes, crossed my tease,
secured beyond a margin joint.

You paragraphed me,
phrased me,
prosed then shaped me.
centred me justified
struck-through me bold.
Then cut and paste, reset me

move-aligned me,
colour-filled in silver-shroud.

Spilt that ink
into my think-tank,
words rumbling tumbled through.
Furious fiction, frantic friction
stumbling, fumbled fresh anew.

And letters tripping letters
skipping alphabet disease,
indented and segmented
italicised with creative ease…

And that little ellipsis heart
just showed me what to ask,
perfecting art of craft and listening
hypnotic task of voice en masse.

You make me want to write and think again,
write and fight some more,
digging deep into crevices of creative cave,
bleeding-breed,
a seed from curious circus-core.
And wanting, scribbling, exploring more.

You've left a precious print on me.
Black sucking scrawls around my heart.
Is it all only words, thousands of little swords,
that surround and suffocate this secret of you?

No vision, no scent, no reality touch.
Tattooed-torrid into my basket mind,
embroidered-ever in my casket kind.

You have shown such a tray of personality scope,
exposed me to their brutal and beauty spirit,
an ocean of discovery provoked for only a moment.

You have such a beautiful soul, yet you damn well
drive me mad, angry, restless, breathless,
then nestled, slight-wrestle, then taking flight.
Perched on different branches as you scream,
me lifting, laughing, lingering on your tender wing.

We have fallen together bold,
sold to slavery script fold.
We are still here
forever written in
Sweet Cyber scold.

The Beautiful Things

(*based on reading* The Butcher Boy *by Patrick McCabe*)

All the beautiful things of the world,
I had been wrong about them.
They meant everything to me.
They were the only things that meant anything at all:

Ma, Da, Joe and Alo.

Then there were the children playing in the lane,
the craic of hacking back frozen puddles and
the comic-book craze and riverside daze.
Flash Bars and Da's trumpet stout,
our John Wayne pout and fairy cakes.
And Ma's snowdrops with their little bone china heads
and skies… skies the colour of oranges.

Ma, Da, Joe and Alo.

I was the boy on the back of the colouring book –
the boy who could walk forever –
the incredible Francie Brady: the Time Lord and
Not A Bad Bastard anymore!

Whee-hoo!

Us Bradys – we'll show them!
We'll show them we can stick together!
Okay, fellas, we're riding out!
Yamma, yamma, yamma!

I fell asleep.

I dreamed I was Bird Who Soars gliding Over The Waves

past the cake-mix fake of crunchy town,
the Bubble house of sow-sent frown,
the maddened squeal of saints and clowns,
the trickle stick of bogmen sounds…

But, in my dream they didn't even know who I was:

Ma, Da, Joe and Alo.

They didn't know the nightmare scare and
Nugent smear,
the goldfish stink and alien jeer,
the fawning scones and tiddly-wink pawn,
the lies and eyes and flies well drawn,
the maggot laugh and cock-Roche pill,
the apples, battles, shit and spill…
They didn't know.

Fucky, wucky, ticky, tocky!

Can you hear me?
(*But I didn't know what I wanted them to hear.*)

CAN YOU HEAR ME?

'Shusssssssssssssssssh!' said the sea.
'Shusssssssssssssssssh!' said the talking bird.
'Shusssssssssssssssssh!' says I.

I'll never leave you, Da.
We're gonna be a happy family. I'll make sure we are!
And Ma?
If I ever have a sweetheart,
I'll tell her the truth and never let her down.
I promise!

The Incredible Francie Brady!
(*It was all up to me now.*)
Francie Brady – Not A Bad Bastard Anymore!
(*Indeed. Me and nobody else.*)

I thought of them lying together – The Lovers:
Ma and Da –
on the pink candlewick bedspread in Bundoran
and I knew they were both thinking of the same things:
all the beautiful things in the world.

Ma – put the moon in your pocket!
Da – play a fine trumpet tune!
Joe – we're still blood brothers and Top of The World!
Alo – tell Mary ye love her. We know ye do!

Are all the beautiful things of this world just lies?
No. They account for everything.

And The Emerald Gems of Ireland?
Everything!

And what about Mrs Nugent?
Nugent? There is ugliness in every beauty, beauty in every ugliness.
Truth in lies that lie in truth.

But you're just a boy with a black hole in his stomach
from not being able to cry out or cry out loud?
I cried out!

And the boy in the colouring book with no colour at all?
I've been coloured: tainted and tortured,
staked and slaughtered!

Orange peel and apple sty, Butcher Boy has gotta cry!
Orange squeal and apple spy, Butcher Boy has gotta die!

I know...

But Ma and Da are waiting for me.
The fruits of my evil have set me free:

'*Oh make my grave large wide and deep*
Put a marble stone at my head and feet
And in the middle a turtle dove
That the world may know I [lived] for love.'

Whenever You Want

no-one ever
dreams about you,
talks around you,
cares for you,
whenever you want them to.

no-one ever
feels for you,
thinks of you,
loves like you,
whenever you want them to.

no-one ever
understands the real you,
laughs with you,
smiles on you,
whenever you want them to.

Strange how it is
because
whenever you want them to –
you never know that I do.

FOG

A soft day tomorrow when gossamer
threads cover the ground
*Lá bog amárach ma chlúdaíonn
téada an phúca an talamh*

It is a sign of good weather when
the dew is still on the grass two
hours after daybreak
*Sioneann agus an drúcht gan leá dhá
uair an chloig tar éis éiri gréine*

If the hedgehog is not seen
before a moonlit night in May
soft, foggy days are due
*Nuair nach bhfeictear an ghráinneog
go dtí oicheanta gealaí i lár
Bealtaine: aimsir bhog cheoch*

This Fear Of Gods

Season of horror hurled hurricane
dug deep our sordid secrets,
our blood spoilt trees
withered,
smothered pistol shaped leaves
left hanging in angry embittered warfare winds,
once served us murderers
cold cathedral hymns.
Now wash our stench from this rot deceit,
story eaten beaten defeat.
Turn our city lights white,
NOT orange,
NOT green,
NO more shades or stripes or emblems seen.

You came here unsuspecting of my land and lie in wait.

I come with wild dirty dogged confession at history heels,
took the tattoo trail to mountain top,
daggered choir crop.
Stung a solitary star, bared solid, barred stare.
Knew a promise of silence there –
No poison cloud or bottled flood or petrolled head.
No faceless crowd, no jagged carved-out carcass shed.

But I feared our world was sinking.

Troubled thinking,
terrorist stink.

Yet,
the dead, they tell no lies.
Boiled stories bold,

they understood *our* Nation –
Toiled and sold.

And you, with voodoo visitation,
all the Gods blown in our path,
one by one,
in the space of a breath,
strangled all hesitation.
Can't undo.
No Act of Contrition!

And voices veiled frail from beyond.
Young boys coiled, buried and soiled.

We *lived* it.
LIVE with it.

But you'll *not* break me,
forsake me, subtract or divide me
cold.

And we *will* change it.

We are hours yet to be counted,
moments to be made and mounted.
Celestial on pedestal with fresh feet of clay.
And hands once cup-fisted like stone –
Birth-earthed open.

Yet winds and
tides driven once by bitter men, and
faithless women, and
families killed in hell harbours and
shipwrecked lives.

I want to pull us out!

I want us to sail free,
berthed on shore of angel wing!
I want us to be strong.
I want no wrong.
I want us to bend like branches shaking guilty song.

We'll walk on water, my love.

Who cares what it means!
Everything is beautiful, and
we are burning, hot.
Light us up.
Strike it!

And we will rise from battered ashes, and this
tightness of tears.

Fierceness of fighting years will
fall from fast faces like sorry rashes,
And words of prescribed prayer –
Buried graces.

Us scarlet with intentions to break down
crosses,
cross borders,
curse hate on cruel corners, and
crimson creep our freedom fossils.

And ghosts of past
raising glasses.
toasting our recovery,
a heart-sworn discovery
of a
new world,

unfurled, and
deserving.

What Gods of tomorrow will
create addictions,
steal gold,
a chalice of harmony drunk, and
peace poured?

Us!
Us glow of green souls
released.
Orange unleashed.
A purity of purpose, and
humanity restored.

So, I ask you:

Seek with fired bulletless eyes.
Taste with tough tongues, thirsting truth.
NO bombed blast bastard kill,
NO more.

NO more ugly anchored army core.
Surrender your scream now to sweet karma.

But those tender ties that bind us, that
bound us, that
once blinded us and
bled us as children.

And preachers, politicians, people, sins,
demonised us,
criminalised us,
demoralised us within.
NO MORE!

Now barricaded behind,
barbed wire blunt.
Perish this past pain, this
sacred shame.

You see, I've come here to meet you –
Not cheat you, beat or delete you.

Let us leave this benediction.
Share communion of unity,
one community.

Bury the stained culture vultures that
destroyed our skin.
Build new altars for our sons and daughters,
pure with every colour, faith, flesh and bone.

NO more fear of other Gods, or guns or protest fogs.
NO more hurt, dagger dirt or hurried hidden hugs.

Let's give it a chance.
Change this strange sorrow,
For our Gods of tomorrow –

Your heart,
my soul,
our open minds to:

Forgive, love, respect, beauty, pride, peace.

Embrace LIVING History. A *new* Peace.

So, take this Fenian hand, dear friend, and
welcome to the other side.

Something Wonderful

It was good driving across the border to Buncrana.
Good to taste sound beer and sharp wit.
It was good meeting a Moville madman and
a joint in his flat with the goldfish and Harry.
It was good the way we got lost and
laughed at strangers in an empty bar.
Deep voices, short skirts, nice toilets.
An hour, a few hours,
taking off as we'd walked in.

It was good that we left and landed in another place,
where everyone else lived where we stood.
It was good that out of three ladies only
one of us got a ladder in her tights.
Good that we looked good, felt good,
but weren't particularly good.

Ahh, but it was wonderful to see you again –
Blue eyes like bottled glass.
Black hair like seaweed mass.

I didn't expect you to talk when you didn't speak.
You were solidly cool.
You were silently calm.
A shadow from the past.

You kissed me,
knowing what I always knew,
that I'll never know to have you.

Wonderful to meet you again.
And aye, it was sad the way the weather changed,
the way night and day traded off and
I went home.

Almost There

A cluster of girls gathered on the dance floor in front of him. Tall, fat, short, thin shapes; dancing, butts out, moving in circular motion, galvanic orange-tinged limbs swaying without inhibition, unchained and free as they never would be in daylight. The fierceness of their glares matched by that of their joy; yellow-to-white teeth bared. Flashing laser lights picking up the dust and curdling smoke, reflecting rings in ears, noses and lips. All James could do was just stare in amazement.

Outnumbered, he made his way to the bar and ordered a double. *Being single wasn't easy*, he thought.

Junk Mail

Hey,

You're nothing but a pot-noodled,
cream-crackered, dead letterhead,
with your brillo-padded dreams and
your peanut-butter spread.
You may lick, you may stamp, you're a First Class sucker,
tear me from this juke-box thud and junk-mail clutter.
Put a stamp to this now as I'm no friend or lender,
just reseal my flaps and return to sender!

Tearingly so,

Angry Envelope,
No Fixed Abode.

Duet Of Mirrored Lovers

The world is fantastic.
It is the ultimate absurd circus
and I am shot from a cannon
into this electrifying energy,
shooting for maximum intensity.

This ray of oneness,
piercing the solitude,
falling bodies on the
ecstasy of flesh.

We were like two stars in the
one consolation.
We had heat,
passion,
fire.

We owe it to ourselves to
fuse together at least
once in ashes,
bitter-sweet perfection,
like dogs of lust and
leashes of memory...

Verbal Veins

The weekend before Christmas
you dropped into my palm
handed me loveliness, shook time, gorgeous calm
beat me at pool, shared some beers,
spilled a street-side kiss
a beautiful legend tripped up by intrigue
stung foreign into tongue and history seek
shared a Bogside pint and in between sheets
of music, warmth, whistle and wink, I
sank into you, I dared you to think

we should never have met
but we did, in the snow
and we laughed and
fell into the wildness of glow
of feeling so right yet wrong place, wrong time
twisting our fingers in curls and in rhyme

but I never did see your hand-written scrawl
as we ink-trapped our thoughts online and in fall
yet I yearned for the curve
of your letters wrapped round mine
but the fear of worldly web deceit
was too much of a crime.

The Mistress

Eight pounds, three ounces she was, and so beautiful: a shock of curly red hair, smooth porcelain skin and rose-petalled cheeks. He could hold her in the palm of his hand, her chubby little fingers opening up like a lily. And her face, oh, her face, was exactly how he had imagined angels to look, and with the bluest of eyes. Like little stars they were. She even had the scent of flowers on her soft skin. She was all Danny's. His own creation. A little piece of heaven, and he would keep his word: he'd tell the wife.

Off My Trolley? You Can Bank On It!

Our relationship has become strained over the years. We've had our ups and downs, for better, for worse, for richer and poorer. But today I am smug. It's payday. My energy is revitalised and I'm on a spree with a skip, spend and shop.

I pay a visit to Mr Banks – the hole-in-the-wall. He may well call the shots but he can't tell me that I have *Insufficient Funds* and spit my card out in disgust. He can't tell me 'no' as he is the bank that likes to say 'yes'. I allow Banksy his spurt of silly questions and ping of orders. I've nothing to fear. I'm in control. I'm not going to lose my head; I'm well balanced. It says so on my pay-slip. All credit is due as I'm perfectly calm.

Insert Card. Okay…

Please Wait. Well, I'm not going anywhere.

I press the correct buttons, hum a tune, tap my foot and wait. Any second now and I'm sorted – or so I think. I gently finger-punch my amount request for the third time. Money talks so I whisper politely, 'Please, give me some money, Mr Banks. I'm a law-abiding citizen. I worked hard for this dosh. I was nice to that snotty Ms Jones the other day. I've earned it. There's a chain of ever-readies with their little cards and pin numbers piling up behind me. Hey, Banksy, purleeese, hurry up!'

But that miserable, mean, horrible, nasty, cruel *bleep* eats my card – MY card! Whole! Smacks his man-mad, grease-goosed lips, belches discreetly, and with one smooth, gliding movement of his greedy plastic panel snaps my hand. Talk about biting the hand that feeds you! I'm seeing red. Blood red. Folk are tutting but I compose myself, ever the lady, and smile, 'Oh, it was the wrong card. How stupid of me!' Well, let's see about that.

I march into the bank and confront a cashier.

'I'm sorry, but your card has expired. There's a shiny new one in the post that will give you more options...'

I don't want options; I want my income! She offers me a weak smile but I demand hard cash. She hesitates, uncertain, but finally relents. Holding back a new obscenity, I take the money and run. It's time to shop 'til I flop.

Soon I am in the aisles of the damned, venturing into the super-wacky world of butter and beans. Must remember the tomatoes, the potatoes, cheese and peas. The bog roll, the swiss roll, some quiche and bleach…

Honestly, we should be provided with elbow, head and kneepads at the local supermarket. And a store map. I'm fed up receiving bruises from joyriding trolleys with no sense of direction, plus I can't find the right brand, the right size, shape, price or the Bisto granules.

But those shoppers that sneak through the Ten Items Only checkout, brazenly flaunting the fact that they have only seven items (I counted them) or are well over the limit (I counted them, too), rile me. Decent law-abiding people (yes, me) pay attention. I have been known to purchase anything up to four unwanted items in order to fulfil the requested quota of Ten Items Only: batteries, tights, plants, yes – even a mop.

Then there's the old dear who insists that the 'three-for-the-price-of-two' packets of toilet paper (with nine rolls per pack) for her laxative-dependent hubby – who she married eighty years ago and who can only use peach-coloured, lightly-scented paper (the hubby, that is) – really only counts as ONE item.

So, do the 'buy-one-get-one-free items (aka BOG OFF)' count as one or two? Is a six-pack a single item? What about Gillette twin blades and multi-strength washing powder? And what about the triple-chocolate chip cookies? And rice and sugar and toothpicks, and then there's the 20% Extra Free? And why is it that beer, peanut butter and Bisto are not closer to the till? Oh, am I being a little bit too pedantic? No, of course not. I'm 100% calm.

Maybe I should be more like my brother – he shops online. Mind you, I did have to lend him a few dessert spoons recently as he was having some friends round. Told him he could keep them – the spoons, that is – but I'm going to get him some new ones. Some shiny versatile new ones. I'm going to buy them in a set rather than separate and cause havoc next time I'm in town. I'm going to open the packaging, take out a fork, accidentally poke someone with it and just pretend that my hand slipped. Yes, just like what that mean Mister Banks did to me. Priceless.

Ahh, the trails and trials of weakly shopping. Whoever said that patience was a virtue was certainly not on cue, had a clue or been in a queue. I may be well spent, stressed out and broke but at least I'm home free and alive.

See, I told you I was calm... well, 99% of the time.

Fancy A Ride?

Although not fortunate enough to possess my own vehicle – not even a pair of roller skates – I still like to travel. After all, a change of scenery is as good as a rest. But why is it that buses take the change and taxies take the rest? Is there any fare that is fair?

Every bus depot has a terminally ill timetable. It's against the rules for a bus to leave, or arrive, on time. It would upset the entire schedule and where would we be then?

You all know the feeling when you want to take the weight off your feet, but have to wait on the street, before your bum meets a seat and you get going. Destination anywhere, east or west, I'll pay my share. (I want to be home before the cows come home, one way or the udder.) All aboard (if you can get that far) for the Magical Mystery Tour. Just how long will it be before we reach our wits' end?

Then there's the subtle brinkmanship of would-be passengers at the kerbside challenging for the ultimate, pole position. Surely that apple-cheeked grandma in the yellow tea-cosy hat wouldn't thump you with her umbrella if you stepped in front of her as the bus arrives on time only fifteen minutes late? Or that nice pin-striped, brief-nutcase wouldn't dare elbow you in the face when you have waited patiently in turn?

Not forgetting, of course, the character who will sweetly sicken you with a smile so you let him push in front of you. The one who always manages to get the best seat, when only ten minutes ago that particular individual was twenty people behind you in the queue.

And the female ones, long-legged and slim, who slither discreetly past while you are left tackling the rest of the scrum, drowning in a sea of arms and legs, bodies and bags, bustling bus-ward?

Suddenly, the bus driver howls, 'Sorry, that's it, we're full!'

Damn right that's it! Don't I feel like a fool!

Two hours and ten tantrums later, normal service resumes with a smile. At last I board the last bus, relieved but bored. We are finally on and off and running. A journey of self-discovery in style through many a mile begins. I seek a seat among my fellow weary-wayside-warriors packed in like hay in a bale, huffing and puffing, shoved in like turkey stuffing. I find my solitude with twisted springs and overflowing ashtray and contemplate a rest in peace… NOT!

Beads of sweat, smelly feet, sweet wrappers, fizzy drinks, rustling papers: what a treat! The noisy and irritating humdrum of someone's Walkman up too loud – it shouldn't be allowed!

The compulsive runny nose behind you sneezes into your shirt collar, and the other one in front spreads back his seat knocking your knees to your chest. You watch his curls twist and turn, sweat and swirl, on the back of his neck. Your shoe stuck to the floor with pink bubblegum. And the reflection of the person, two seats down, watching them self in the window, watching you watching them and picking their nose. The young couple opposite feeling each other up as if I didn't know what they're up to. Stirrings, secret shivers and smiles spill the beans.

It's mean to be travelling alone, you and your world inside one weekend bag, crammed into seven square inches of space worse than any confessional box or rundown telephone kiosk. Your neck hurts, your rear end uncomfortably numb and your legs like comatosed Mexican rubber. And so much for the armrests! They dig into your ribs and jolt you upright like a lollipop that's lost its flavour. Your stomach turns inside out as another legendary Irish pothole sends you and your bladder into utter turmoil.

Don't want to read, can't sleep, fed up with staring out blankly at balls of wool and milk-machines in twirling fields. The scenery just flashes by and you develop a hot, bewildering flush. Temper flares as wain-with-sticky-fingers pulls your hair (in an attempt to scalp you) and screams with frustration as nature calls. One of the giggling brat pack down the back pukes into a plastic Tesco's bag and the aroma of last night's adventure wavers up for your approval.

A quick pee and a well-deserved smoke at the halfway stop. Dishwater tea and lack of bog roll. Supposed solace for the soul. A ten-minute break for sanity's sake. How much more of this can one possibly take? Then squeeze and tumble into the rumble of the Contraption of Catastrophe to be tangled up in the jungle of bags and feet all over again. The show is on the road. This road. Going nowhere fast enough.

The bus driver doesn't give a hoot. He likes to tell people where to get off. Well, stop the world *I* want to get off! Oh, how I yearn for trains, planes and automobiles. The Wheels of Fortune, if I were fortunate enough.

Maybe next time, I'll get happy with a taxi (or in a taxi) on a road less travelled and a mind less razzled.

Take it from me. Take a hike. Get on your bike or let your fingers do the walking. In the meantime, I'm learning to drive!

FROST

If the blackbirds call at dusk there
will be a sharp chill at night
Fuacht anocht go tobann an lon dub
hag déanamh ceoil mara bheadh
cloigín miotail á bhualadh

Are We History?

My heart and I
pack a rucksack of
gold kisses in proud green rain.
How I read to you,
you played with my hair,
you drew my portrait,
I painted yours.
You brought me daffodils, breakfast,
I wore your socks,
you stole mine.
Odd they were then,
odd we are now…

We'd meet in corner bars,
hide from army crouch alert,
scribble dirt doodles,
score words, firing our flesh and
tongues torrid up against the city walls.
And shots of cheap warm cider, brandy,
Sundays sweet with sinning pleasure,
terrified into tempestuous chaos,
and did not answer the phone.

I gave you Sinatra...
You showed me broken town,
that petrol-bombed youth,
mine; village cartoon frown.

We threw coppers into jukeboxes,
danced in street moonlit riot,
me laughing; scared at gun-slung shadow.
You taught me how to play pool,
to fight back: No Surrender!

Snooker the bastards,
sink the orange pink.

Then gutted hopes.
Black streets with secrets.
Marched cold and angry to Bogside corner,
January thirtieth every year.
And we'd get drunk and shock with stories
of those who remembered,
and I'd shiver.
I never spoke.
You wouldn't listen.

You were drawn to the voice of my mother,
talked history, politics, religion, war.
Dad and I tried the *Irish Times* crossword,
scolding bold dog-scratch on solid oak chair.

Yes, it's your birthday today,
I know. I've known for the last eleven years.
The first four, God, how I loved you…
The next three were pretty good.
Then two blew into somewhere
but last year?
I don't remember,
and today – I couldn't care.

Cast

Your soul shone stark
like slither of fish skin.
My stung tears,
dead salty,
heart sunken
deep wanted dug
out to soak
with tadpole stroke
but
you stood proud
on false shore,
diseased rock, as
I fought against
your selfish tide
and drowned.

Distance

Between us:

Twelve pound fifty
One hour and forty minutes
One taxi (*maybe a bus*)
A front door
A flatmate
A skin colour
An accent
Musical taste
A lighter (*or would you prefer a match?*)
Different drinks
Different faiths
Different circumstances...
Nah, it would never work

(*See you next Tuesday*)

Love Bug

For a long time
my heart skipped a beat when I saw a red car.
I never knew the registration or make
but I knew the engine snore and the car-door creak.
I knew the comfort of the passenger seat,
I knew the chaotic contents of the boot and floor.
I got used to the character and adored our little trips.
And I loved you,
but you drove me away.
So I don't look for red cars any more;
I search for green.

T-EX-T

i cradle da mobile
lik a butterfly caught
we flex + we tex
r secretive thoughts

i re-read
ur 1st
ur 2nd
ur 3rd

lukin 4 clues
somethin absurd

da codes dat we send
arrive ona dance
fingers flutter n flurry
flirtin w chance

i imagine ur thumb
shift at da beep
i imagine ur hand
consider delete

i imagine da night
shud voices replace
i imagine da site
of ur hidden face

but da spell will b broken
once voices r shared
shuda kept us so quiet
as a txt can b herd

Imagine This

a voice
a face –
what gives
chase?

a number
a trace –
what paves
grace?

decision
precision
incision
dance

derision
confusion
illusion
chance

how can you miss something you've never known?
how can you kiss someone you've never been shown?

imagine,
imagine...

it could be so beautiful
it could be a crime
she has the imagination
but does he have the time?

Imagine that!

Just A Tic

Patriotic,
Rhetoric,
Apologetic?
NEVER.

Cathartic,
Hedonistic,
Lethargic?
NO.

Ironic,
Chronic,
Symbolic?
PERHAPS.

Amused,
Confused,
Used?

WHO CARES?

Tuppence Worth

I guess I've always wondered
Standing cold at a bus stop
If I blew my cigarette hard enough, hot enough
I'd melt these fluffy snowflakes
With the smoke
All over your perfect painted face or
Even wipe you out.

Then stamp all over the slushy blob
As I fished out all my saved coppers
On the arrival of the long-awaited bus.

Like A Charm

A sinister moon hung like a suicide's scream over the deadly heat of a thousand lustful sins and secrets. Tonight, she would charm again.

She wore a blood-red coral bracelet of seven beads, signifying the seven deadly sins. By sunrise, she will have destroyed one man, one sin from the chain. Strangers had fallen in love with her. She'd lure them deep to her seductive curse. Their sexual greed was her salvation; a total surrender with no remorse. But why should she suffer alone? They had infected her.

Now she would give them back a little.

Call it Gift Aid.

Isn't It Swell?

You drank my secrets
I poured them in
I gave you prose pearls
You tore their rim
You didn't drench me
Bathe true with soul
So I shall go now
Salt goodbye-kiss
Let waves caress me
Give love a miss.

End Of The Line

I have been traced through my gender's grace, pinned down strong in this female race. I have had that purple star stapled to my heart. I am a woman whose cradle waits for her womb to grow with sons and daughters of wind and rain. This is me. Look at me. Ready to breed. Ready to seed with another generation.

I anxiously wait for him to answer. That white coat. Grey face.

'Erm, Mrs Childers, I am so very, very sorry…'

I crush the little pink booties in my mind. Blood, finger, scissors. End of the line. History. Her story. Mine.

Tomato Soup

It was the best-before date that made me remember.
The keep-stored-until and use-by date.
And I remembered our first date:
the stirrings of love and selection,
the spaghetti confetti of connection…
God, it was delicious as we ate.

But the taste didn't last.
You preferred fish.
Bowled over sideways,
bold broken dish.

So I'm very careful about what I choose to bite.
And I'm very wary of my appetite,
be it rhubarb, custard, green eggs and ham,
I sure as hell won't be beaten by the can.

STORM

A storm will come when
seagulls fly inward
Nuair a thiocfaidh na faoileáin
faoin sliabh tiocfaidh an
stoirm ina ndiaidh

A calm night often makes
a stormy morning
Cothú na doininne
soineannn na hoíche

A faint wind forecasts thunder
Gaoth leamh na toirní

Darkness And Light

The strange man and his black dog were just a few yards behind me. My hands were shaking. Anxiety stormed through my shivering bones. I cowered while the rain slapped my scalp and whipped my face as if angry. Dark clouds hung viciously above trees like ogres with arms outstretched. I rattled raw beneath their scary skeleton-like fingers and began to panic. It was killing me. I could smell it. Taste it. I couldn't prolong it any more. This was the only chance I had left… I had to face him.

'Excuse me, mister. Have ye gotta light?' I wheezed.

Storm

Your eyes like a stormy night
vinyl streets, magic light score,
anxious, torrential, midnight blue pour
pulse, swell, overcast, soak
fill with hot liquid stroke
engrossed, raw, dare to choke

Mine rain, shower moon, shriek stare
beg for rush gush, rainbow dance flare
shadow cast hot, rivered, ablaze
tongue thunder tripped,
lightening streak crazed.

Crashing like stars
avalanched bound,
volcanic depth charged
kiss hiss drizzle singed.

Then morning, clouds lift,
a-glistened, rays breeze,
and we shine,
forgive night and thirst for release.

Invasion

Beat her good and proper last night. Slashed his bastard tool between her thighs: thumping, pumped. Ranting rage. Panties torn. She lay there exposed: raw, bleeding, broken. Numbed inside. Eyes pleading, *please, no*!

Cover the face. Shield the spit. Don't cry. For God's sake, don't whimper. Ten minutes, it's done. Then fast asleep, drunk, forgotten. Be strong. Think of the kids… your marriage… his family… Let him have it. Let it be.

You see, this is how he cares, is showing you his love. Just another Saturday night. No-one will ever know.

'Are you all right there, my love?'

Love Sick

Feverish thickness, deadly disease
Spreading your sex germs, sleazy spit sneeze
Coughing up love-lust phlegm
Rash resins, riled romance
Wounds worry stab-sore stung
Epidemic cursed chance.

Heart gorged, blood-boiled poisoned
Raped mind, whoring out
Measled thoughts of tomorrow
Brained, stained, skinned, boned, gout.

Paranoid parasites passion penetrate
Medicinal maggots hunger hived head
Contagious
Outrageous
Violently-spermed
Fatal
Pre-natal
War-whipped womb, flesh turned.

You fucked life
You sucked death
Devil bastard
Migraine led
Thigh tonic
Calves chronic
Brutal birth babe
Drop dead:

Love.

A Piece Of Work

Imprisoned by blood ink-spill
because of just him
he buckles my being
won't let me begin

wants me for his wanting
his dinner
washing up
cruel breath on my breathing
poured poison
murdered cup

no interest in woman
no love for my art
just cruelty and anger
and bitch-bite remarked

trapped by his temper
chained to his heart
fingered and face-plucked
tortured and smart

kicked into slave roll
supply on demand
never fresh or just sober
served bold to his hand

evil-eyed and tongue-snarled
dare drunk on his spit
lie lifeless and limbless
curled, cornered and clipped

comedy of belonging
he screws with my mind
fictitious flesh rendered
blind me from behind

leer mocking at tears drawn
get off on my fright
Alpha Adonis Ass-Hole
disgusting delight

ragged and wretched
let you come on my skin
polluted, perverted
bruise bullied further in

sharp glint in this nightmare
dreamt order to cease
shock quietly, stab quickly
Now *I* May Have Peace...

Marmalade Madman

The sheer shape of you
tickles my eyes and teases my nerve.
A bundle of rags, a fistful of fags,
cherishing the dares of slags and hags,
shagging and bragging about the old bags.

Dragging their flat-bums out of the chat-slums,
humming thin tunes under slim moons,
spooning dead wit and spinning bullshit,
knitting the fools with their drools and barstools.

A stinker, a drinker, a wanker, a winker,
a lanky pink unthankful thinker,
a minty, kinky, darling charmer,
some ego, amigo, performer, alarmer.

A weekend offender, an insane pretender,
blending and lending yet bending untender,
well-spent and hell bent on any swell gender,
gent rent and frequent; rough rider, rude render.

And hoovering, manoeuvring, canoodling, user.
A sleeper, a creeper, a cheapskate, abuser.
A nutcase, a headcase, a shit face, a loooooser.

Then hubbing, and rubbing, club-loving disgracer,
and chasing, defacing, female-stalk pacing.
Farting and flirting, curt-larking, jerk lurking.
Aye, thanking, yeah yanking – a party spit spanking.
To mock, to mortify, to minimise, then scrutinize.

But the rest of the best, (blessed with full breast),
them dippy, hip-slippy, hot lippy confessed,

grow with the flow of your dirty dog glow,
falling, ball-crawling with circus-slap show.

As you feed on the need of the deed of your seed
achieving your weaving by greeding your reed –
It isn't your RIGHT!
It isn't your CALL!
DON'T call me a bird, a babe or a doll!
Those thoughts in your head should never be said
because one of these days, MATE,
you'll be fucked dead in bed!

The Second Coming

First Confession:

You preyed on me,
I prayed for you
on bended knees
twisted limbed degrees.
Our sorry souls
begged forgiveness;
release.
Recreated in an image,
Christ creased.

My Holy Communion:

I hummed for Him,
His hymn on hive,
alive in me.
He took me,
gave thanks,
broke me
gave to me.
Did this in
Remembrance of
Him.
And I drank tongue,
sucked sinners' skin,
templed brim.

This beauty an altar –
full of grace,
on devil worship wing,
hot angelic blood,
chorused flood,

burst-cursing, devout.

An act of contrition;
Repeat,
Repent...
It is All God's Love
love, love, love...
And I am sin.

The Confirmation:

Nailed me,
cross-tossed
bled me.
His Kingdom came.
Took my name in vain.
Done to me
not done to others.
As it is in Him,
through Him,
with Him,
in Him,
me on Him.

Heaven on Earth,
rebirthed,
blessed,
chalice fisted,
hallelujah kissed it,
parted red sea.

Commandments broken,
demanded,
stroken.
fruit tasted,

souls sold,
flesh unwasted,
guilt bold.

Erected,
genuflect.
Protected,
resurrect.
Connected,
eject...

Let Us All Stand:

This is a Gift from God.
You are my Saviour.
We will rise again,
sin again.

And I,
Amongst women,
And you,
Adamned man,
must amend
this
Amen.

Brutal B&B

Thin veiled bones of birds
fallen death from air
overcast little skeletons,
it's happenin' everywhere:

It's happenin' in the streets
broken shells beaten weep,
racking wounds, crackle blast,
fisted flesh, carcass cast,
amputation, condemnation,
disfiguration of love and limbs.
Incinerated, mutilated,
boy-toy soldier's triggered sins.

Sneak jeep-leaping into creeping
of bloody baggy body heaps,
static smack, whack-attack,
children burn, as shrapnel sleeps.

A place of sand, divided hands,
friends now enemies,
nightmare rent.
A place of mothers, fathers, brothers,
lullabies: eulogies,
lives are spent.

And the bodies found,
and the bodies counted,
and the bodies bound,
and the bodies mounted,
BOMBED from the skies,
BOMBED in disguise,
BOMBED in despise

from the rise
of power and greed,
– some fuckin' creed –
yet... unborn babies bleed.

Death is such an easy word to pronounce.
Just say it again and again and again.
Death rhymes with breath,
last breath: first breath,
death breath...

As distant observers we speak,
without guilt.
We speak without fear.
We speak without knowledge.
Our misplaced honour on humanity core.
As royal loyalties blow in thrusts and gusts of
spit and dirt and shit and hurt and hate alert –
We sit and cool.

WE SIT and fool ourselves that it's not here.
It's there.
What do we care?

But the war is on the kitchen table.
The-war-is-on-the-kitchen-table
egging to be read.
Begging us to wake up, to wise up!
My coffee black as buildings:
churned, collapsed, shot... and thousands dead.

I load my spoon with sugar,
dissolving, percolated brains.

I stir, swallow, smear over screeching headlines
that will not, that do not, disappear.

I bite, chew, choke as images outline
a starving world on rage and war.

I flick the page to daily horoscopes:
scoop the horror of appetite apartheid,
as sons and daughters in crusts of homes,
wafer-towns, deserted bones,
shattered souls and sores in doorways,
hearts and minds exposed in more ways.

My coffee cold as I heat in anger,
my conscience rots to feed a hunger,
to fuel a need to stop all hate,
too cruel the deeds of religious gait –
the puppet politics of no man's fate.

And the bodies found,
and the bodies counted,
and the bodies bound,
and the bodies mounted,
BOMBED from the skies,
BOMBED in disguise,
BOMBED in despise
from the rise
of power and greed,
– some fuckin' creed –
yet… unborn babies bleed.

The taste of all this sours human tongue.
For *my* name? this is NOT done.
I've read an' dread over sight and word,
colours of all pollute our world.
diluting faiths is not the game –

JESUS CHRIST, ALLAH, BUDDHA:
Hell – We ALL bleed this shame.

Bus STOP!

You stand innocent.
Preoccupied with the night. Wednesday night.
Safe with your own company.
Minding your own business.
Annoying no-one.
Waiting for the last bus home.

City drunks stagger by.
You light up another cigarette.
In this darkness you think you are alone yet a young
courting couple close by.
You feel safe. Hum a tune.
Chew gum. Befriend their shadows.
Chew some more.
Drag, puff, cough.
Drum-de-dum.

Smell a mixture of aftershave. Alcohol. Something un-
clear.
Some footsteps imagined.
Hear slurred canned laughter.
Sneered smear.
Distant hostile cheer.

Young couple beside copulate, fornicate, investigate.
Warm moonlight caresses obvious, *oblivious.*
Shrill-drill of their beauty undress.

Then –

A stranger's breath.
Sudden spit.
Foul and damp.

Deep in my mouth.
Holding a body that looks like mine.
Does not speak but his eyes glint like knives.
I taste the blood he wants as I bite my lip.
I *think* I scream but the night remains silently intact,
unlike me –
Swallowed gum, swollen gum.

Gravel and glass slice bare breasts.
Stones graze neck in mock affection.
Frozen blue with cold-chilled fear.
Grabs faster...

Someone please hear

Only heat coming sickeningly from him.
My wet. Silent. Sore. Tear of tears.
My knickers down.
His dick up.
Buttons undone.
Clothes dappled with blood.
Dark hair streaked with mud.
Finger clawed-spread.
Cruel full moon spotlights me,
colouring my skin thickly pale.
Big Mac and urine perfume the air.
Grow cold inside as my thighs burn with shame.

I woman.
I victim.
I'm dead. To blame.

Courting couple sing, laugh, smile over.
I stare scarred. Strangle glare. *Dare* them to look back.
They don't. I can't.

I hurt, I fold.
He grins; my skin.
His sin. He goes…

I stand gutless.
Unoccupied with the night.
Wednesday night.
Disgusted with my own company.
Knowing my own business.
Telling no-one.
Waiting, *waiting* for that last bus home…

Under Cover

You were there. I could feel you inside but I couldn't tell them. I couldn't tell him – the shame, the disgust, the fear. I booked a return ticket to London. It was two days before my birthday. I was nineteen.

'Visiting friends,' I'd said. 'Just for the weekend. Will bring you back something.'

And I did: my empty womb.

SNOW

The day that melts the snow
Lá coscartha an tsneachta

Have a drop of the hard stuff
and make a fool of the cold
Bíodh braon agat chun amadán
a dhéanamh den fhuacht

An Eve With Myself

My mind stands ajar, an undressed drawer
lined with forgotten words,
waiting for the important one,
as the cradle waits
for the womb to be done.

'Let me sleep with him,' I ask,
as women begin to stem into trees
their breasts sprouting leaves,
blossoms falling,
sheltering under your wing,
to spring forth with autumnal glow,
wintering bright on summer show.

Three sisters arrived on the rays of the moon.
Three sons bellied forth from your furnished room.
And it was you
who gave me wide woman hips,
balanced each side like two halves of apple.
But I am too fragile
to give all love to just one soul.
Show me how –
this truth from pain,
a peace to gain,
full fruit in basket
procreation game.

I have learned from you,
holding arms high in creative air.
I have cried for you,
folding harms away to sedative care.

I have been traced through with gender grace.

I have been pinned down, proud female face.
I have had a purple star stapled to my heart.
I have not yet rode upon the apple cart.

Is this where I belong, where
clasped futures are not yet born?

I tempt a bite,
remove pips of doubt
and shut the door.

Silver Sister

Someone stole the leaf from
your branch and
scratched the bark from
your tree.

How I wanted and wished for your happiness.
Evergreen, ever more, even more.
Your secret garden, your diligent dreams.

Rain and wind pelted,
snapped and stabbed your soul.
Yet, sun and moon,
gorgeous touch on your face,
saved you.

More new, more hue, more you.
Fed and flowered with colour,
you sowed your seeds of promise,

And me – just knowing a handful of your buds;
me, just growing with the loveliness of you.

Sweet sister –

I will water you,
I will trim those evils from your path,
I will preen you to perfection and
I will love you always.

Twin Peeks

You were always better at numbers
at scrunching up Tayto crisps to not share,
at charming your way out of trouble and
always had better hair.

Born of an Easter Sunday,
for years we were dressed; me in pink, you in blue,
these colours matched birthday cakes until
our 18th and 21st –
where your half was iced like a pint glass
while mine remained rose-budded and shmoo.

We shared First Communion and Confirmation,
shared the donations and bought new shoes, and at
National School had to sit beside each other
when the rest of the class got to choose.

You taught me how to catch tadpoles,
squash spiders into matchboxes and sail.
You taught me how to play Monopoly,
although you always sent me straight to jail.

As teenagers we'd match-make our friends,
we always knew who fancied who –
The advantages of having a twin sibling
although you always had a later curfew.

Now as adults we're separated by city,
furthered by status and truth.
As adults we don't see or talk much and
I yearn for the yarn of our youth.

The blackberry picking and squabbling,

the times you stuck up for me at school,
Saturday nights out at Scamps with our peers, and
me always beating you at pool

I forgive you for drowning my first teddy,
I forgive you for telling me Santa wasn't true,
I forgive you for throwing me in a cowpat,
I forgive you for always wearing blue.

I miss not seeing you as often,
I miss how we used to be,
I just want you to know, little brother,
that you mean the world to me.

For You

They, who are dear to me, do not know
that you, borrowed mile, or thousand moonbeams filed,
are nearer to me than they will ever be

They, who all speak to me, do not know
that my heart is full of whispered, wanton words
that must remain untouched, unspoken, unheard

They, who crowd curve my world, do not know
that I, without dream, thought of you,
breathe sore in longing, loneliness

They, who do blood-love me so, do not know
that my soul sighs silent secret ache
for that which will, still, can never be

They do not know me,
Do you?
Do I?
I do.

Send In The Clowns

He told him where to find her.

'Down by the shore with her sisters,' he said. 'Collecting shells.'

It was 1966 and they were all in love – courting, dancing, the slick-backed hair, the girls in mini-skirts. And laughing.

Michael went to find her. He had bought her a watch as a gift. She was to be the one. His one true love. He was the piano man from Dublin, looked like Fred Astaire, and she a local girl; the second oldest of five siblings: fair-skinned, lightly freckled, blue eyes, raven-haired – a lovely vision with a heart of gold. And all the guys had their girls on their arms in those dusk-dancing parties, thin summer frocks and evenings bright. A gang of about twelve and all in their twenties; twinkling with innocence and that thirst for life.

My dad introduced them. Three fortnights later they were engaged and married on New Year's Eve: white velvet with red roses; it snowed with their warmth. They bore two sons, two daughters and eight grandchildren.

**

I was a bridesmaid at your daughter's wedding. My best friend, Lisa. I'm four months older than her, but none the wiser. Us childhood friends and still as ever today. Those precious links passed down from parents – from you. From my dad.

We've shared our firsts of everything and have still kept our secrets. We've danced and laughed and cried and fallen out and given in and given out and gone to school and so much more. Same as you did, Mrs B. And your daughter looked like an angel on her special day. She looked like you. You were so proud of her. We all were. We still are. I even wore pretty girly shoes under that gold dress instead of the Docs and you said to me, 'Some day, Jenni, you'll stop wearing black!' And I remember it was just before then that I felt old enough to call you by your first name and you laughed as you said we'd never grow up.

That night us women shared a bottle or two of wine and you let me smoke a cigarette at the kitchen table and told us all those funny stories about my dad and how he had chased after my mum. And how when Lisa was born my dad gave you a shiny coin.

That was October. Seven years ago. By Christmas you had cancer.

Everything changed, but by GOD, you were a fighter! Such spirit, such strength, such determination, such faith… You started to really live your life. It was your right! You travelled and shopped and went to see musicals. You volunteered to help the sick and went to Lourdes. You worked with others who shared your illness until you could do no more. But you wouldn't give up and always, *always* had a smile and were positive.

You wouldn't cry. You didn't cry. You let your daughters and sons and Michael believe there was still hope. You never *once* complained or told of the pain. Your pain. Your body weak, your will to fight it courageous, you rising and raging against it.

**

It was raining today. August thirty-first. There was thunder and we all shared umbrellas. You had asked for them to play *Send In The Clowns*. And they did.

By God, those tears were harder than that rain. Nothing could shield them, but it was a beautiful service. Your family and friends all there to say goodbye. You would have loved it, Mrs B. The chapel was full with the scent of roses, yellow and all they were, too. And so very, very strong. You would have been so proud! We're all going to miss you. I'll miss you, and, I promise, I will be there for Lisa – my dear child-to-adulthood friend, Lisa. Yes, I will be there.

And I will smoke another cigarette at your kitchen table and I will still be wearing black and those awful Docs… and you're right, we'll never grow up.

Ye know, you will live on. On with life, in life… in Lisa. In that power of love. All sides of that shimmering coin.

And we, too, will have daughters who will be great friends tomorrow, and in your memory, always and forever… and we shall never, *never* forget to Send In The Clowns.

Mrs B – Rest In Peace x
28 August 2005.

Blue

Tiny mountains of silver dust scatter around me. Green, by a swirl, ruffles trees and grass. Yellow for sunlight and Mummy's hair. Dull brown for boots and puppies' tails, black for cats and scary nights, red for smiles and apples bright. But my favourite, little stubby blue, is for water and sky and the colour that was my Daddy's eyes.

Remembering September

I was in the card shop in Derry, buying a belated birthday card for a friend. The song on the radio fizzled out. The girl behind the counter turned the volume up: *News Flash – Plane just crashed into one of the Twin Towers at the World Trade Centre, New York…*

Shoppers dropped their stance. Stunned silence. This was not a movie trailer. This was real, happening live. A wet Tuesday near 3:00pm.

I got a taxi home and switched on the TV. Another plane had struck the Twin Towers… total confusion, fear, shock. Thought of where Tina, her boyfriend Dermot and her sister Mary were. Knew Tina worked nearby in Pearl Street. Jesus, what the hell was happening?

I switched channels. Every station: grey slabs, skies pulped, smoke-fuelled, fire-gripped as sirens screeched, newscasters gasped… then fade to black. Dust rolls choking skyline. Human flares like scorched confetti. Newsreel rattling death toll. Couldn't breathe. Couldn't speak. Couldn't turn the TV off. Couldn't focus. Fingers fumbling phone. Panic. Couldn't get through. Rang Tina's mum in Shroove. 'The girls are safe.' Thank God. Oh my God. Tears of relief but total disbelief. Cannot comprehend. Terror. Horror. Numb.

Exactly a year previous – 11 September 2000 – I had flown into New York: sunny, fearless, excited, free. We visited the Twin Towers in daylight and reached the Top of the World as the sun went down. Spectacular. Stunned awe. Beyond any movie still. Yet 365 days later – all gone. Some 2,753 lives torched.

In November 2009, I was back in New York. Awake in the wake of the recent past. I was in Fulton Street, where the Strand Book Store used to be. A Japanese tourist asked me for directions to Ground Zero. I pointed west;

just a few streets away. A massive grave full of angels. I couldn't go although I wanted to. I wasn't ready. I said a prayer and offered it up, got the subway back to Queens. Back to Tina and Dermot and their three young sons. Safe. Silent. Surreal.

A decade after the horror and destruction, we shall remember the heroes and helpers, both then and now. We shall remember those who loved and lost, those that never lived to see their children grow up nor bear any of their own, those that live on in memory, hurt, grief, strength and truth. The stars in our global skies are those precious souls wishing us to forgive, heal, live life and seek peace. We might not always see them but they're there. And before we go to sleep tonight – be we in Moville, Manhattan or Melbourne – we shall tell our family that we love them and thank them. We shall weather all storms and shine on.

And I shall visit New York again and quietly, gently, hug her tight and tell her she's among friends and will come home…

A Sort Of Homecoming This Christmas

December 1980

Two weeks before Christmas, we would start counting trees. All six of us.

Crouched in the back of Dad's car, we would silently tip-tap the window, excited little fingerprints veined like butterflies' wings. We'd been up to Derry from across the border to snatch the last of Christmas gifts with our piggy bank coins, stealing secretive peeks at the treasures from brown paper bags. It was well past the smudge of dusk and time to drive home. The promise of homemade mince pies with jagged cloves and the smell of forest pine and cinnamon teased the senses. Mum and family dog were waiting.

From the car window, the mystic silvery-blue ocean held only the shimmering reflection of frosty stars. We sped along, stunned by the rush of sparkling diamond jewels from strangers' darkened front rooms: majestic evergreens bedecked like emperors or little crooked shrubs nobbled with lights, bright and sticky like boiled sweets. Their garlands of dancing fairies, magic carnivals and strands of twinkling tinsel made us wish for angels and mermaids, Father Christmas and footprints deep to jigsaw step in snow. Bedtime couldn't come soon enough...

December 1990

It started – that magical moment – when I ventured from the Big Smoke (Dublin) via the Little Smoke (Derry) to that little curling wisp of heaven by the shore in Inishowen. The trip from the Fair City to the Maiden City to the back door of soul-sweet-home. Temporarily quitting the student life – its existence in the back seat of my mind. Temporarily embracing the social life – its readiness in first gear, revved up, raring to go. Sleigh bells drumming. Twinkle humming. Chums and slumming.

The Christmas I plunged into the darkness of Donegal, the depths of family and massed ranks of former peers. The Christmas I was alive 'n' kicking, rockin' an' rollin', young, free and single; ready, willing and stable under mistletoe and bar stool, well fed with sinful grin.

The Christmas I was lost in the blur of hurried kisses from anyone and everyone in enormous rooms and carolled corners with old adversaries, old best friends, old flames, old fools... The shake, the rattle and the Bacardi rum – mingling and jingling with the thrills and spills of seasonal love, brotherly love, divine love, Christian love, drunken love... Love thy neighbour, love thy postman, love the brother's girlfriend's cousin...

It was the Christmas I was thin, crimson, and viewing everything through contact lenses, then beer goggles to blurry haze – crimson with cheer and festive fearlessness. The glimmering, shimmering gathering of parents and their six little prodigal sons and daughters, no longer dream believers in Father Christmas yet darling believers in a Christmas for parents. (Oh, and firm believers in wild parties, fast sleighs, late nights, long mornings, with a slipped tenner from Da to help.)

There was Quality Street. Sweet quantity of giving and receiving. Unwrapping a gift, to the then sincere shift of a hug, a laugh, a squeal, a dig in the ribs: the Body Shop basket or groovy writing set, the lucky-bag earrings and book already read. The oversized lingerie, the socks, some chocs, a board game. And funny-shaped sweet candles, CDs, perfume, yucky picture frame. Then the good-humoured fight over the purple hazelnut twirl and whose turn it was to check on the dinner, and sipping on Baileys or Brandy or coffee, and sneezing a tease at the twin in Garfield slippers.

Yes, beautiful moments (and they were the moments) spent beside a brilliant tree, a splendid fire rekindling the past (and the ashes), with wine, and chat and the Essential Pavarotti. And slicing the coke with a spray of vodka, cheating at cards and acting the eejit. Paper party hat crowned and pulling silly crackers, and trying to catch *The Sound of Music*.

It was the Christmas I wore red in Greencastle, got merry in Moville and danced to *Tainted Love* in Tul na Rí's disco. The Christmas I fell flat in the snow, moved with the flow, never felt low. It was the Christmas I think I grew up and I loved every minute. I had changed from that sweet-awed innocence of girl in pigtails to one accepting all those around, to love and cherish, to forgive and share and just appreciate and thank my lucky stars for all.

December 2008

Christmas is a time for kids. A time for the used-to-be kids. The kids in wrinkled polished skin. The kids that never became adults, and me. A time when we try to play Happy Families but can't resist the challenge of good arguing time over co-operation (after all, it only defeats the purpose of having siblings, parents, cousins and family dog). But how you adore each and every one of them.

They say that everything about Christmas is wonderful when your age is in single figures, but, trust me, it is twice as magical when the age doubles. The trouble is that this year, for some strange reason, I'm a little more nostalgic, more reflective... and know I'm going to really miss the counting of trees from my father's car, the student seasonal snogs and slip-ups. I'm going to miss that intrigue of childhood excitement, the innocence, the beauty, the warmth, the 4:00am squeals on discovery of Santa's visit.

For some strange reason, I just know that this Christmas is going to be different. My parents aren't getting any younger. Some of my brothers and sisters live elsewhere or abroad. Some will be working or with their own young families. It's my turn to give back to those who made past Christmases so special. And I will.

RAINBOW

When the sun has thin, straggling
legs, bad weather is ahead
An ghrian agus cosa
fúithi – drochshíon

When the sun's legs are up at
morning and down at evening,
the best weather is coming
Toghna na haimsire chugainn –
cosa na gréine suas ar maidin
agus síos tráthnóna

The red moon rises quietly over
the hill and brings good weather
Dea-aimsir an ghealach ag éirí go
socair dearg de dhroim an chnoic

Breathless

Dublin – you're like a very cool cousin with your
buzz, boisterous and bountiful presence.
You sparkle, sweep, shout and speed between the lights.
Derry – the loyal, lovely, big sis with her
familiar, friendly and fashioned ways
as you trip up the streets to twinkle.
And Inishowen – like a warm hug, with the kettle on
and a sofa smile as you unwind, unpack and relish
in the comfort of a quiet hour after hectic
to look forward to the jazz and blush of more.

Lost Weekend

To cool by evening sunset
Rest easy on basking breeze
Teasing jugs of amber juice
Lazing with childhood friends
Gently laughing, letting hair down
Chatting late on twilight dates
Sleeping long and hugging morning
Senses stirred yet wide-awake
Reading, writing, thinking wide
Feelings, dealings, a life aside
Tossing, turning mixed branch of muse
Captive conversation, gorgeous cruise
Wild and free, no clutch of curse
When I tiptoe back September first.

Brisbane Beat

I felt alive again:

The belt of life again,
a story stirred in scent of
turning up and on
of wishing words and throng
of twinning tongues among
across the world sprung from
a little leaf from tree
a tiny bark of me
dragged balconic cigarette
flagged tonic pyro-nette
squealed teens in heels connect
tease fifties dress-etiquette
boy/girl, girl/boy then boy-on-boy
strut-tutted Queensland taxi joy.

A car-park kiss.
An Aussie fist.
A Chinese lisp.
Backpacker twist
outside phone box junk
inside hostel bunk
spy Kiwi pretty hunk
'just twenty-five' he joked
a pint of culture soaked.

Some felt alive, once more
in Brisbane heat adore
on pavement cheat encore
and I just winked a smile
I blinked a chink of guile
of mouth-on-word; agile

unbuckled thoughts dialled home
I fastened night for loan
to postcard memoir roam
a city swept, hot spent
its crazy face on rent
and I stole time...

No Rehearsal

Her face sears, a mask of hot prickles, when people stare. Unseeing strangers. The quiet makes her shiver. She has a sense of herself, twinkling, in that cluster of hushed seconds. Silver screen swells with colour, pulses, hurls light. Upturned faces licked by ghostly beams. Whispers simmer with back-seat parties as secret sensations rise.

There he is: a creature struck stupid by torch-wink. An awesome eye, face whacked angelic with light. Above the shimmer of lips, her eyes sting, stunned. Can he see her?

Everyone folds back into velvet; squirming laughter, creasing faces, oblivious.

First date – no rehearsal.

More Weddings And A Fuddle

It's the first time I'm going to a wedding without parental guidance and pre-napkin (bibbed) agreements. It's the first time that I'm going to a wedding some years partnered, unwed, glad-ragged and high-heeled. It's 1996 and I need the tricks.

Well I've been in love before, danced the salsa, step-walked the waltz, and giggled with Great Uncle Albert at family gatherings before, Mrs Gleeson on his lap. Sipped Football Special and Ice Cream Soda in tall glasses with ice. Played Frisbee with beer mats and laughed loudly at relatives' hats.

That yearly ritual of meeting up with spotty-nosed, freckle-faced cousins from afar. Those memorable acquaintances resulting from births, bereavements and betrothals – the additions, the losses and the wannabe-joined.

Those were the idealistic events when Mum dressed you in pink, ribbons and white ankle socks with patent black shoes. A perfect little darling with front tooth missing and National Health specs. When Dad would laugh in jest at his six- and seven-year-old daughters' future marriages to wealthy, healthy, good-looking gentlemen. Sons-in-law, who would never break the law, but matched a pint and would tread softly on the putting green. No man too good, or good enough, for his three little angels with dirty faces and pig-tailed hair.

Weddings were so much fun then – an adventure and discovery of grown-up life. And I was to marry Cousin Colum from Cork and raise chickens in County Clare. But what on heaven, and on earth, are weddings possibly like now?

Well, for starters, main course and dessert – thank God it's not mine! I have severe indigestion on what to wear. What colour, what length, height, width, shape? Should

I lose weight, gain weight, dye hair or shave hair? What about a handbag, the lipstick, the earrings or a hat trick?

For the last month I've been in constant uncontrollable indecisiveness. I wear the sort of clothes I wear to save me the trouble of deciding what to wear. I base my choice on what doesn't itch, pinch or break the bank balance. I have never had a handbag. Never owned one, borrowed one, bought one or begged for one. As for lipstick – a definite no-go! I genuinely detest the smell and taste of it. I think my lips are red enough without the help of Max Factor or maybe Maybelline. I talk so much the blood flows naturally to my gob and long-lastingly, it works. But I've been practising for weeks around the house in my brand-new shoes. They have a three-inch heel and sound great on carpet, though scare me on tiles. It's the kitchen floor that requires my sure-footedness, or I'll be squatting like a duck at the edge of the dance floor.

But the show must go on... and the shoes, the dress, the make-up and matching handbag; the sheer tights, the dizzy sights, the wiggle, the giggle, the scent and the smile.

It's the day I'll step out of the teenage-held-casual-clothed-years into the twenty-something, laden-look of a lady. A beautiful occasion when two wonderful friends become as one among friends and family in finest glory.

It really is that lovely time of year; the marital bliss of tying the knot. The 'he loves me, he loves me a lot' syndrome. And he does. And I do. But I won't, not just yet!

The Night I Went As A Vodka Bottle

I've been abroad, through the straight and narrow, the thick and thin of it and boogied across the border, but nothing, *nothing*, beats the heat of Hallowe'en in the heart of the North West. Open your eyes, ears and wardrobes to the macabre, inventive and downright hilarity of a Hallowe'en in all its majestic extravagance.

It is a DIY spectacle, on a shoestring budget, worthy of any Hieronymus Bosch masterpiece. Cardboard, double-back sticky tape, tinfoil and bright paints; a Blue Peter special. All art skills put to the test to make daft and crafty creations by the very best dedicated followers of fashion. It is a Rocky Horror Picture Show of homemade, one-night-stand costumes with best-before-dates to last until dawn (or *with* Dawn if you can find her). It is a truth set in the stones of the city's wailing walls.

If any stranger (or spirit for that matter) should ever ask you what makes this night in our historic city on the Foyle unique and outstanding, well, it has to be the Derry folk. Come along and witness the witches, warriors and warlocks in all shapes and sizes. Seize your soul and introduce it to the night of all nights and the delight of all figures and frights. Get ready to rock, shock and have your eyes roll with a howling wind and earthshaking fireworks. Marvel and march aboard the Maiden City's magical mystery tour.

Ecstatic faces of children, painted and perfect in autumnal glow, shine and shiver with endless bewilderment, clenching tightly their parents' grasp. Yet it is their elders who steal the power and glory from what is universally regarded as an occasion for the youngsters. After the illuminating array of sky darts, the real horrors of the night begin to surface. When the rest of the world is calming itself into a secret slumber, Derry gathers itself into a storm of fantastic frenzy.

It has to be one of the best nights to be young, free and single. To have fun, scream and mingle. Those brief encounters of any kind or close encounters with any briefs. Forget the What Not To Wear duo. Shimmy on those pink fishnet tights, don Miss Piggy's wig and be outstanding with Dolly's chest. It may be men behaving badly, but sometimes looking better.

It is the night for the good, the bad and the blood-beer thirsty. And flesh, no longer confined to the bed/bathroom, is bared against the cold, frosty chill of this October night, warmed only by the alcohol and other people's enthusiasm.

It is an electric atmosphere of grinning reapers, rockers in frocks and all the usual suspects. A rage of originality with iconic characters and a reservoir of hippies, pirates, medics and dogs. Where thirty-something-year-old men strut along the Strand Road in nine-inch cerise stilettos, with guys and dolls, dressed as cheap coppers, drinking on the job. Humanised household appliances and makeshift toothpaste tubes squeeze their charm on giggling schoolgirls who are more enamoured with the cast of *Braveheart* lookalikes. It is a night complemented by meeting and making new friends, sharing the craziness and the enigmatic experience of the seasoned spell.

A shower of rain washes face paint, glitter and soggy cardboard down the length of Shipquay Street as it all comes to an end, and so, too, the costumes. Bleary-eyed yet content, smudged faces and squeaky footwear wander and wobble over to taxi queues and saunter homeward. Rising early for work the next morning is far from our minds. I will pray for the delivery of us all from the evils of the night before until that morning has broken.

I remember so well one of the first great Hallowe'en

nights I shared in the city of crazies and one of the wackiest (and ultimately embarrassing) costumes I ever mashed together. You see, it was one of those life-size, blow-up, Vodka Doll publicity balloon things – not unlike a blow-up doll, I presume (although I've never seen such delectable dollies). I had acquired it from an off-licence in town (for why or what originally, who knows?). It was see-through and had the Smirnoff logo stamped into the plastic. So I grabbed the Vodka Doll, unfastened its plug and released the trapped air, then cut off the top for a hat and the bottom. Coat hangers wired around both rims gave it that cylinder-like shape and then I lined the inner plastic with white cloth. I climbed in and there I was: Miss Smug-Off Vodka 1995. A friend painted my face (all white with mini logo) and we hit the bars.

Christ, it was bloody hot sealed in plastic and any beer spillage rippled over the coat-hangered edge and over me. You could say I had the scent of what I was – an alcoholic beverage – and down to a tea. It got cigarette burns that left gaping holes, and the smell...

We were having a hooley and a bit of a laugh, kicking heels, singing and enjoying the craic, in generally high spooky spirits. I got a bit knackered so I perched one buttock half on a stool (I couldn't really sit down with the coat hangers) near a blazing fire. After a while, rested, I got up to boogie my way to the toilets and aggghhh! Where the feck's my back gone? The whole bleeding thing had melted, disintegrated, shrivelled up! Curled bits of stinking plastic stuck to the stool, my hand, my pint, my hair... my embarrASSment, my shame, my disgust... Me crying, me drunk, me melted... Like that witch out of the feckin' *Wizard Of Oz*!

I had to quickly take the damn thing off and accidentally stabbed a friend with the crooked coat hanger; white cloth all stained with spillages and smoke burns. I wasn't allowed to turf the plastic piece into the fire and watch it sizzle so had to carry the stinking thing around with me for the rest of the night. I pretended that I was some sort of ghost, although by then it looked like a stained bog roll. The shame. Plastic Fantastic. Never again!

So over the years I've been a cigarette (which looked more like a traumatised toilet brush), a pint of Guinness, that melting bottle of vodka, a cave woman and a vampiress-like tramp. All homemade creations and gone now forever. As, too, is my reputation. But it was all in the name of good, clean, only-to-be-had-in-Derry-on-Hallowe'en FUN!

Mine's A Carlsberg

Are you any of the following?

(a) The curvaceous, hourglass, body-beautiful with legs like telegraph poles
(b) Dating a barman/barmaid or are one of their mates
(c) Holding a fifty-pound note as if it were a cigarette
(d) A visiting Head of State, or
(e) None of the above?

For me, at this moment only, I'm just a little 'e', and I eff-ing deserve to get zzzonked out on the Alphabet Street of love, lunacy and luminosity.

Meeting the girls for a mad night out. Crazy ladies dolled up and on the pull: a cocktail of belly laughs and buddy-babble. On the town, down the pub and there we are. And yet, it really is an ordeal to venture for service equipped only with that tenner and that wicked smile.

Confronted by boys on stools and girls in heels, stretched like a police cordon the whole length of the bar. Is it justice or is it just me? Sweaty yet sincere: rich dudes, pretty faces, closed ranks denying spaces. I'm disgraced at the pace of obtaining a drink in this place. Each one of us clambers for the bar rail as if it were the deck rail on a sinking ship. Women and children, with fake ID, first. Blood is thicker than water. Beer is thicker than blood. Either way, sorrows will inevitably be drowned.

I'm squashed against some smelly-breathed, big-foot-ed, gaping young lager-lout with no manners or morals. I receive a bang on the ear, a slap on the rear, dear God, bring on the beer. The three behind the bar see not, hear not, speak not. My growls in the midst of this barbaric jungle-juice struggle. I can taste it, tiger-tongue thirsty, I just have to get wasted.

Suddenly, I land on my feet, eagle-eyed. Just one small step and a kind hand to the side: a giant leap for my state of mind. Ahh, but not quite! The bum in the cardi breezes by me as the jock with the Rolling Rock knocks me back. Shaken and stirred, but certainly not slurred, I glare up at the pair. How do they dare? The sadist, the masochist, and wee 'me', a pacifist? And then I am there at the bar for that jar.

The barman gives me a nasty look. I didn't need it. I already had one. But pleased as punch, I demanded my cure:

'Two Guinness, please!'

'Ach, sorry… (*Pure genius, the keg has run out. This can't be good for you at any price. Now, steady on, Jen, settle your head.*) How's about Smithwicks, love?'

'Erm, no thanks.'

'Bass?'

'I'll pass…'

'What d'you want, then?'

'Carlsberg. Two. Probably the best.'

I hop and skip through the mobs of dedicated followers, scotch-free. No sooner got and money spent, the beer is down and the truth, and gut, is out. I go through the same rites of passage, again and again, for another and another. Sea legs gained, I follow the flow of the river to the sea. Numbed by the rum and the fun of it all. Taking the rough with the smooth, the cool with the lukewarm, the flat with the settled, the good, the bad and the damn-right ugly. Seeing double and feeling single, I order triple and have a quibble. Giving lip with the more I sip. But I am not so think as you drunk I am.

Escape to the Ladies, go there to be seen, trade one farce for another, social event of the evening. Travelling in packs of three to the loo: one to pee, one to pose, whatever is due. A little lipstick, a lot of life, a bit of slander, then hairspray strife. All great craic with the stirring of high-heels, clickity-clack with ceramic-tiled ease. Smiling sweetly, yet hardly sincere, this maiden with manners, waiting in fear. Yearning for natural relief behind doors, more grief at reflection in make-up smudged mirrors: a beauty and beast to beget and behold, boisterously bursting and beautifully bold.

We've got to remember, us girls on the tear, we've got to be quick, to get a seat there. No waiting around, no matter how keen, don't get your knickers in a twist, just make sure you've been.

Then the last shout for the last pint – the bell tolls, the drum rolls. We are thrown, bodies and coats, into the night with the fright of cold air and a fearful fare. Corralled into the pick 'n' mix of dudes and chicks, smells and fells of drunken pricks, hunks and chunks of taxi queues. It's getting late, it's time to make tracks, join the end of the queue, but these are the facts: there's the fight to stay, the right of way, the discussion on who's paying or should we stray?

There's Kevin and Sharon, Tracy and Marvin, Shaz and Dave, Paddy and his babe. There's the ladies and tramps, the beauties and beasts, handbags and beer-cans, hot-smelling feasts. Queuing with this midnight mode will never put us on the road because Kevin's buddy John is also coming along and frog-jumps the queue and forgets about you. When you're standing still in line, some think that it's fine to start chatting you up when you'd rather they'd stop:

'Hey, ye on yer own? Want me to take ye home? Going to Culmore?'

'But they'll only take four…'

'Well, then, you and yer mate? Fancy more than a date?'

'But my boyfriend, his sister, her cousin, their neighbour?'

'And rumour has it there's a rave up in Rosemount at number five, sure the night is still young, still single and alive… and did ye hear about yer wan who works and on the dole? Now, I'm telling ye in confidence, so don't tell a soul… and yer wan in the suit is married with a wain, what the hell is he doing with Mike's girlfriend Jane? Did ye see what she's wearing, all fluffy an' pink? Sure ye wouldn't use that to wipe down the sink! So, how's about me and you, and where d'ye say yer off to?'

A taxi beeps, that's me for keeps and safe at last, I grab the back seat; relieved and relaxed, take the wait off my feet. Oh, let's talk about the weather and the new shopping centre. Let's talk about the news and the price of kids' shoes. Let me bitch about my work and that pedigree jerk. And the No Smoking policy and the taxi man's philosophy. And as for tonight – ye wouldn't believe the… sight.

So, have I spent my time wisely or let myself down? Should I have chosen a night in or out on the town?

I don't care for telly and going to bed early. I don't care for quiet and the latest diet. I don't care to save a pound when the girls are around. I like where I am and I don't give a damn. In a bar I can burp, I can flirt, I can drawl. I can dish the dirt. I can wear that skirt. I can laugh and drink. I can sit and think. Some of my best achievements are as a result of this. It's a hit or miss. You get the gist. No kiss and tell, ahh, but it was swell.

So I'll harp on about that another time, 'cause in the meantime, I've got mine, and mine's a Carlsberg. Cheers!

Water Dance

I am rain
stream
waterfall
creek and river
waves, sea and ocean

I am mist
fog
cloud
frost
ice
snow
storm

I am rainbow

Follow me…